ABOUT THE BOOK

The idea for writing this book seemed to me like a natural progression from the writing of individual tutorials. It allows me to place the various skill levels in order, offering a starting platform for the complete novice, through to the more advanced levels, as well as giving ideas for more experienced wireworkers to develop their existing abilities.

The book offers a step-by-step guide to getting started, which includes some of the tools and materials available, and gets progressively more challenging through each section. **Each project teaches you new skills and techniques so, as with any form of instruction, before you begin work it is important to read the book from start to finish, so that you do not miss anything important.**

My vision for the book is that it is purely focused on wirework. Due to the fact that cold connections are used and only a minimal amount of tools, the set-up cost to get started is quite low. There is also a full section of jewelry findings, so that you can make these too, thus saving on the amount of materials you need to invest in to complete the projects.

The projects are very detailed, leaving no guesswork, so that any reader is able to complete all the projects successfully. The main focus of the book is on wire weaving, binding, coiling and layering.

Although there are many different shapes and sizes of wire available, I have designed all of the projects using five types of wire throughout the whole book, again this reduces the initial investment required to complete the designs.

I have poured all of my jewelry-making knowledge and skills – built up over many years – into this book to provide a comprehensive guide. So I guess you could say it is a lifetime of research!

CONTENTS

WIRE JEWELRY

WRAPPED, COILED AND WOVEN PIECES USING FINE MATERIALS

MASTERCLASS

ABBY HOOK

GUILD OF MASTER
CRAFTSMAN PUBLICATIONS

First published 2011 by
Guild of Master Craftsman Publications Ltd
Castle Place, 166 High Street, Lewes,
East Sussex BN7 1XU

Text © Abby Hook, 2011
Copyright in the Work © GMC Publications Ltd, 2011

ISBN 978-1-86108-842-0

Publisher: Jonathan Bailey
Production Manager: Jim Bulley
Managing Editor: Gerrie Purcell
Senior Project Editor: Wendy McAngus
Editor: Judith Chamberlain-Webber
Managing Art Editor: Gilda Pacitti
Photographers: Tim Clinch and Abby Hook
Designer: Chloë Alexander

Set in Interstate and Trajan
Colour origination by GMC Reprographics
Printed and bound by Hing Yip Printing Co. Ltd in China.

TOOLS AND MATERIALS

In this section I introduce the items required to make wire jewelry. First we look at tools, where I outline the essentials and then go on to describe the ones that will make your life easier. From there we move on to wire: the different types available, their properties and some of the pros and cons.

TOOLS

ESSENTIAL TOOLS

There are many different types of tools on the market that can help you with your wirework.
The list of various pliers that are now available is endless, particularly when you look at
the range of forming pliers on the market. I don't tend to use these as I think any wirework
requires just six essential tools. Always buy the best you can afford though; the better
quality the tools, the longer they will last – they will also make your life much easier.

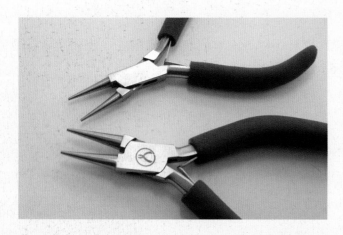

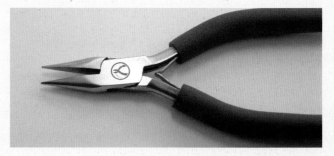

▲ **Round-nose pliers** The jaws should be perfectly round and
smooth. They should taper to a fine point, to allow you to make
tiny loops. They are used to make loops and swirls but not to hold
the wire as they will mark it with small divots.

▼ **Flat-nose pliers** These should be perfectly flat inside the jaw,
so that they do not mark the wire when you grasp it. They should
also have straight sides and top edge. They are used to grip the
wire and to make clean, sharp bends.

▲ **Chain-nose pliers** (also known as long-nose) As with flat-nose
pliers, they should have a smooth, flat inner jaw, while the outer
edge should be curved. The jaw should be tapered. Used to grip
the wire, they are also very important for tucking wire ends in, as
with their narrow tip and flat inner edge, they are able to access
difficult places within your wirework.

▼ **Nylon-jaw pliers** You can get round-nose and flat-nose nylon
jaw pliers, but the essential type is flat-nose. This strange looking
tool is very useful – by running wire through the closed jaw you
can easily straighten and/or harden the wire. You can also flatten
shapes and small frames by squeezing them between the jaws.
The beauty of these pliers is that they will not mark even the
softest of wire. The only drawback is that they do not have
the best grip on the wire.

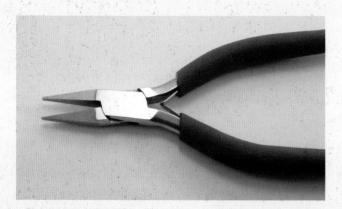

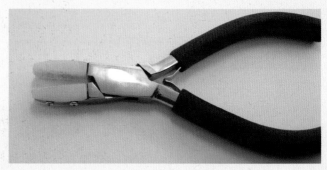

Tape measure/ruler I find a tape measure easier to use than a ruler because its flexibility means you can shape it around items. If you do not have one available, you can put a piece of string around the item and then measure the string against the ruler.

▶ **Wire cutters** There are two main types available:
- Flush cutters (also known as side cutters)
- End cutters

I recommend using flush cutters, as you are able to get much closer to the wirework with these. It is also important to mention that the jaws must meet perfectly, forming a flat edge on one side when closed. When you use this side to cut, the end of the wire will be perfectly flush, with no sharp points. The better quality cutters you buy, the less sanding you will have to do.

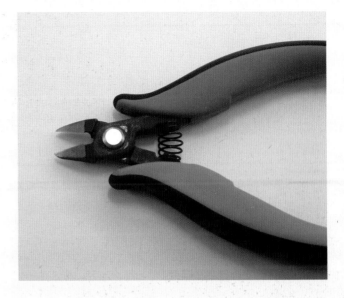

Handling your tools

It is also important to note that the handles are a vital part of your tools. You will be spending a lot of time holding them, so they need to be comfortable and easy to grip.

With your pliers, the most effective way to hold them is to grasp one of the handles between your thumb and forefinger, pulling the end of the handle into the palm of your hand to stabilise the pliers. This leaves your other three fingers free to move the other jaw, allowing tiny, controlled movements, without applying a death grip!

Always be aware of the position of your hands and wrists. Do not over stretch. It is far better to reposition the pliers than to over stretch your wrist.

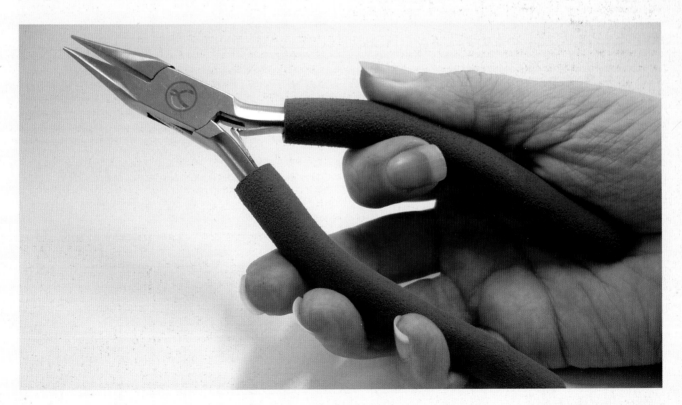

ADDITIONAL TOOLS

Remember that you can sometimes find inexpensive or even free alternatives to some tools with a little imagination. For example, before buying my steel-tapered oval bracelet mandrel, I used an old table leg to shape my cuffs for years! Kebab skewers, old pens or knitting needles are perfect for shaping bail wires around – just experiment a little.

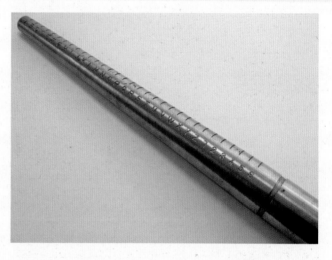

▲ **Hammer (chasing or goldsmith's)** Used with the anvil to flatten and/or texture the wire. The goldsmith's hammer is the correct tool to use for this, but I prefer a chasing hammer, as it has one flat side (with curved edges, so you do not dent the wire) and one curved or ball end, which is great for creating texture.

▼ **Anvil or metal block** Used to hammer against. It is important that it is perfectly smooth, so that you do not mark the wire at all. If you don't have an anvil, a smooth, flat metal object could be used instead.

▲ **Ring mandrel** Stepped and tapered – and sized – these are used to shape the wire, generally used for ring shanks but they are also useful whenever a smooth curve is required.

▼ **Bracelet mandrel** These are round and oval and, as the name suggests, used to shape wire around for bracelets and cuffs.

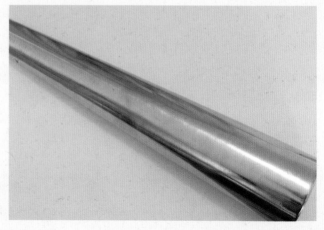

▲ **Rawhide mallet** For hardening the wire without marking or flattening it. Also useful to help you shape wire around mandrels, hammering it in to place.

Bead reamer Used to enlarge bead holes, although you can use a round needle file instead.

Bead board A very useful and inexpensive addition to your tool kit. Typically they have several compartments, along with grooves which allow you to lay out your designs.

Jigs There are many types of jig on the market and they are generally a Perspex board with holes drilled at regular intervals with removable steel pegs. While they help you make consistent shapes they can be quite restrictive. I have found it is far better to master the pliers!

Tumbler Used to polish and harden finished pieces. Steel shot and detergent are added to the barrel along with the item of jewelry to be polished.

Bench clamp A useful tool for holding your mandrels in place while you work.

Safety goggles/glasses Be careful when snipping wire ends, as they can ping anywhere. You can cover the wire end with your hand when cutting but it is far safer to wear goggles - you only have one pair of eyes - take care of them!

▶ **File/needle files** These are for smoothing wire ends and enlarging bead holes.

▲ **Sanding pads** If you mark the wire, you can sand the marks out by starting with the roughest grit (the most abrasive) and working down to the finest. I use sponge sanding pads, as they are soft and flexible and you can wash them after use, so they last a long time.

I use the following grits:
- Grain size 180 – Fine
- Grain size 220 – Extra fine
- Grain size 280 – Ultra fine

Light (to work under) It is important that your work space is well lit; you do not want to strain your eyes!

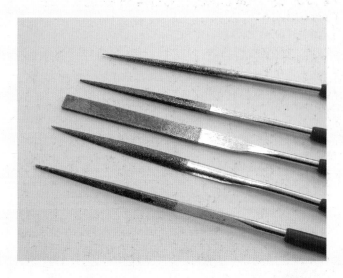

Protractor To measure the angle of your bends in the wire to ensure accurate shaping.

▶ **Polishing cloths** I use cloths that have been impregnated with a cleaning and anti-tarnish agent. All that's needed is a gentle rub of your silver from time to time to maintain the shine. Do not wash and it will last for ages. In the absence of polishing cloths, you can use a very small amount of toothpaste (not gel) with a soft nylon brush (an old clean tooth brush will do) or cotton pad – be sure to clean all the toothpaste off afterwards though!

Masking tape Also known as decorators' tape, this is useful when you have multiple structure wires, as it helps to keep everything in position while you work, but still allows you to move the piece around freely, unlike a bench clamp (it is cheaper too!). As it is a low-tack sticking tape it does not leave residue on the wire.

MATERIALS

WIRE

Wire comes in a whole array of shapes, sizes and metals. Although I tend to concentrate on the wire types that you will need to be familiar with in order to complete the various projects in this book, I also describe other types on the market and some of the terms used. There is also a section of handy hints and tips to help you on your way.

TYPES OF WIRE

Learning to work with wire can be an expensive process. When you first start you will find that you get through a lot of wire, just learning the basic techniques. This can be all the more frustrating if you are working with precious metals, as every mistake is an expensive one. I always recommend that when you are learning or trying out a new technique that you work first with 'practice wire' so that you can move onto precious metals with confidence.

Practice wire

▶ **Copper wire** This is readily available, cheap and easy to work with, making it most people's first choice as a practice wire. It is currently enjoying a resurgence, with many jewelry makers using this as their preferred medium due to both its cost and its attractive colour. Bear in mind though that when copper comes into contact with skin it will discolour. There are sealing products on the market but I have not tried them myself and they need to be reapplied as they do wear off. You can reduce the amount copper discolours by oxidising it. This is a permanent effect.

Artistic wire Very cheap and available in myriad colours allowing you to create vibrant, playful pieces. As with the others though, this is generally coated copper wire and the coating will wear off.

There are many other types of metal you could use, including brass and bronze; they are not quite as cheap as copper but still less expensive than silver or gold.

Precious metals

Sterling silver This is my wire of choice. It is normally 92.5% silver and 7.5% other metals (usually copper), which makes it stronger than fine silver and able to withstand the manipulation of coiling and weaving without snapping. However, because of the mixed metal content, it will tarnish with time and so it does need to be cleaned regularly to keep it looking its best. It is available in round, half round and square in the full range of hardnesses and sizes.

Fine silver This is generally 99.9% pure silver. It is very soft - too soft for a lot of wirework projects. It is great when working with a torch though, and very easy to use if you are creating balled ends or for use with solder.

Argentium silver The main advantage is its low tarnish. It is still an alloy but some of the copper has been replaced with germanium.

Gold This is not a metal I tend to work with, purely because of personal preference - I love silver! Gold wire is available in all the same sizes and shapes, although it is a lot more expensive.

Platinum Fast becoming the holy grail of wire for wire workers, it retains all the beauty of silver but with added value. New products in platinum are being introduced all the time.

SIZE AND HARDNESS OF WIRE

The sizes I have detailed below are the ones I have used in the book. There are a whole array of other sizes available.

28-gauge or 0.315mm Very, very thin wire; used for coiling and weaving; not suitable as structure wire.

24-gauge or 0.5mm Great for binding or wrapping briolettes; can be used for spirals as long as they are not supportive.

20-gauge or 0.8mm Used mainly for creating spirals and wire details; can also be used for structures when there are other supporting wires available.

▲▼ **Silver/gold plated wire** This is easy to get hold of and also cheap. It is generally copper wire with a thin sterling silver or gold layer. It is easy to work with and initially looks great, but with time and wear the silver or gold coating comes off, leaving the copper exposed, which compromises the overall look of your design.

18-gauge or 1mm Used as structure wire.

16-gauge or 1.2mm Used as a structure wire; also for clasps.

The gauges I have given here are AWG (American Wire Gauge), which is the gauge most people work to. The other alternative is SWG (Standard Wire Gauge) and you can easily find comparison charts online if needed.

There are three different hardnesses for wire; the one you choose to work with is really up to personal preference.

Soft As the name suggests, soft wire is very pliable and easy to shape. It takes longer to work harden and is therefore less likely to snap, however it does not tend to hold its shape as well as the others and generally requires hardening once your design is complete.

Half-hard This is the hardness I generally work with – it is the happy medium as it is soft enough to be able to shape without too much trouble and yet hard enough to hold its shape.

Hard This is very hard – too hard for me to work with, but for some designs that need to be very rigid whilst you are working on them, you may want to consider this option.

There are also different shapes available, these are commonly round, half round and square. For the purposes of this book I have used only round.

WORKING WITH WIRE

Here are some notes and tips to help you when working with wire:

1 Try not to work with more than 30in (76cm) of 28-gauge wire at a time, to avoid kinks, snapping and generally getting in a tangle.

2 Copper and sterling silver are very different to work with. Copper is far more pliable and silver work hardens more quickly.

3 When you have finished making your jewelry, wash it with a tiny amount of washing-up liquid. (Or mix up a bottle with a few drops of detergent and half fill with water. Shake well to mix.) Make sure you rinse it thoroughly and see it sparkle. This will remove any oils left on the wire from your hands, reducing oxidisation and discolouration.

4 Repetition is the best method of practice.

5 Patience is the name of the game; take your time and never rush! That is when mistakes happen.

6 Save all your off-cuts of wire for recycling – most suppliers will buy back wire, saving you money.

7 Polish copper with a gold polishing cloth to bring it to a high shine and reduce oxidisation.

8 It is better to cut the wire too long than too short; it is very frustrating if you run out at a crucial point and off-cuts can be used to make findings.

9 Your movements with the wire should be smooth and even to avoid kinks and snapping.

10 It is better to start with the correct length of coiling wire to avoid having to connect a new one, but sometimes this is unavoidable. In these cases there are two ways of attaching a new one.
● Coil the old wire until you are $\frac{1}{2}$in–1in (1cm–2.5cm) from the end, trim to a taper and crimp into place. Cut a new length of wire and – leaving a 1in (2.5cm) tail to hold onto – attach three to four coils from the end of the old one, lock the new coils into place between the old ones and then continue as before. Once the new wire is secure, trim to a taper and crimp into place. Ensure that the ends of the wires are on the inside of your wirework, so that they are hidden.
● Alternatively, you can slightly flatten the ends of the old and new wires, trim them to a taper, so that they overlap each other slightly and crimp into place. The flattening of the wire will result in the overlap being the same thickness as the round wire.

OXIDIZERS

There are many products available for oxidizing your finished pieces. This is a great way to highlight the detail in very ornate pieces and works particularly well with wire weaving.

Liver of Sulphur (LOS) This is a concentrated chemical that smells like bad eggs. You can either get it in a crystal form, which you dissolve in warm water, or a concentrated liquid that you dilute. You need to either heat the solution or the piece that you want to oxidize for it to work effectively. It is also important that the item is perfectly clean before you start this procedure, otherwise it will not work properly. The longer you leave the jewelry in the solution the darker it will go.

Once you have reached the desired colour, carefully remove the piece from the solution. To obtain a very dark colour, simply rub the jewelry item all over with a polishing cloth, returning all of the raised points to a high shine and leaving all the recessed areas dark. Alternatively, you can rub the whole piece with steel wool or a scouring pad and then polish. This will return the raised areas to a brilliant silver (or copper) colour, depending on your wire.

The drawback with using LOS is the amount of cleaning your jewelry requires afterwards and disposing of the solution – the following option eliminates these problems and is more environmentally friendly for pretty much the same results.

Boiled egg Yes, you can really permanently oxidize your jewelry with a hardboiled egg! Simply hard boil an egg, chop it into quarters and pop it into a small airtight plastic container (don't bother removing the shell), along with your jewelry and wait until it cools. It only has an effect while the egg is hot, so if your jewelry is not quite dark enough once the egg has cooled, simply microwave it for a couple of seconds to warm it up again, remembering to remove the jewelry first! Then clean the piece in the same way as with LOS.

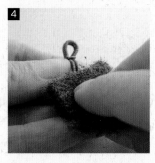

1 Hard boil an egg, cut it into quarters and pop it into a small airtight container with your piece of jewelry.

2 Once the egg has cooled your piece of jewelry will have changed from this...

3 ...to this.

4 Rub your jewelry with a scouring pad to return the raised areas to their original colour.

5 Polish to finish.

FINDINGS AND BASIC TECHNIQUES

This section teaches you how to make all the findings you will need to make your own jewelry.

Each project also covers some of the basic techniques you will use in the rest of the book, so it is important that you get to grips with these before moving on to the next section.

This book will take you from the basics through to advanced levels, so the projects get progressively more challenging.

Below is a list of the findings and the techniques covered:

Simple earwires
- Forming a simple wire shape
- Forming a round loop
- Getting to grips with pliers
- Straightening wire with nylon-jaw pliers

Coiled earwires
- Coiling with thin wire

Figure-of-eight links and chain
- Making consistent-sized loops

Wrapped link and chain
- Making a secure wrapped loop
- Adding beads

Coiled wire cone
- Precision placement of wire

Headpin and bead dangle
- Making your own headpin

Wrapped briolette or drop
- Hiding wire ends

Brooch pin
- Accurate shaping and forming

Hook and 'S' clasp
- Shaping and hammering wire

Simple T-bar and toggle clasp
- Shaping thick wire
- Forming a ring
- Hammering a section of the finished piece

Coiled T-bar and toggle clasp
- Attaching a thin wire to the frame
- Binding to add strength and detail

SIMPLE EARWIRES

You can create your own earwires from a single piece of wire – they are quick to make and easy to use.

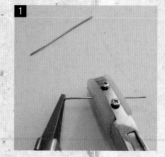
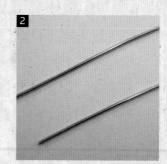

Materials (for one pair)
- 3in (7.5cm) 20-gauge soft or half-hard round wire

Tools
- Round-nose pliers
- Flat-nose pliers
- Nylon-jaw pliers
- Flush-wire cutters
- File or sanding pads
- Tape measure

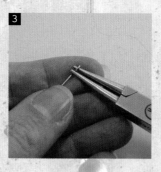
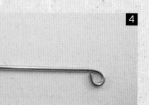

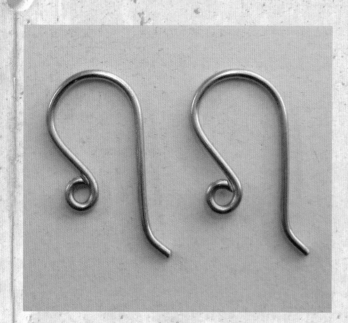

1 Prepare the wire
Cut two pieces of 20-gauge wire, each 1½in (4cm). Straighten the wire by holding one end in your flat-nose pliers and pulling the wire through the jaws of the nylon-jaw pliers.

2 This will straighten the wire so that it is ready to use. It will also harden the wire slightly, so that the earwires will hold their shape. Repeat on the second piece of wire.

3 Form a loop
Grasp the end of one piece of wire with your round-nose pliers. Holding the wire in place with one hand, turn the pliers, so the wire wraps around the jaw to form a loop. **Tip:** Never squeeze too tightly when using the round-nose pliers as you will leave divots in the wire.

4 Repeat on the other piece of wire.

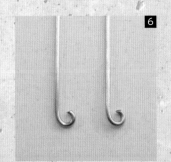

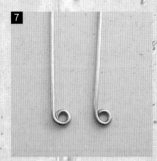

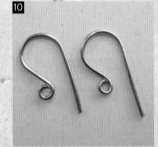

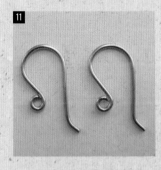

5 Make the loops round
At this point we have two egg-shaped loops. In order to make them round, snip the top corner off the end of the wire, by positioning the wire cutters as shown.

6 Notice how this opens the loop up.

7 Close the loops with your round-nose pliers so that the end of the wire sits tightly against the straight length. Repeat on the other piece of wire.

8 Form the hook
Grasp the straight wire with the thickest part of the jaw of the round-nose pliers, just above the loop.

9 Wrap the straight wire around the jaw of the pliers, forming a hook shape.

10 Repeat on the second piece of wire.

11 Final step
Grasp the end of the wire with your flat-nose pliers and bend upwards by 45°. File or sand the end so that there are no sharp edges. Give the earwire a squeeze between the nylon-jaw pliers to flatten and harden the wire. Repeat on the second piece of wire.

COILED EARWIRES

Ever wondered how to make your own professional-looking earwires? This project shows you how. One of the many advantages of this design is that you can co-ordinate the earwire with your earring design, by using a matching bead. It is also a great way to use up some of those off-cuts of 20- and 28-gauge wires!

Materials (for one pair)
- 4in (10cm) 20-gauge soft or half-hard round wire
- 3in (7.5cm) 28-gauge soft or half-hard round wire
- Two ¹⁄₁₆in (2mm) beads

Tools
- Chain-nose pliers
- Round-nose pliers
- Flat-nose pliers
- Nylon-jaw pliers
- Wire cutters
- File/sanding pads
- Hammer (optional)
- Anvil (optional)
- Tape measure

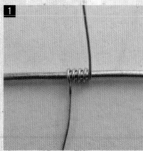

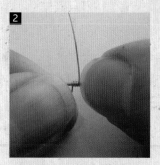

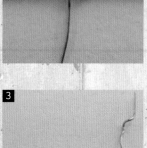

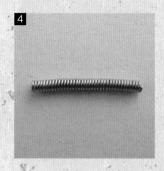

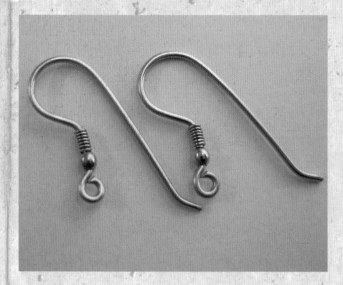

1 Preparation
Take a piece of 28-gauge wire (the off-cut used here is 6in/ 15cm long). Use either an off-cut of 20-gauge wire as a mandrel, or cut a new piece 2in (5cm) long (this can be used for the actual earwire later). Coil the 28-gauge wire around the 20-gauge one, leaving a 1in (2.5cm) tail (use this to hold the wire in place while coiling). Keep the 28-gauge wire at a 90° angle to the 20-gauge wire at all times to ensure the coiling is straight and neat.
Tip: I make these earwires to use up 28-gauge wire off-cuts, so I prepare the coils first, winding lengths of wire then chopping the coils to length. As a rule, you will use 1in (2.5cm) of 28-gauge wire per seven coils, when wrapping round 20-gauge wire.

2 Every five or six coils slide your thumbnail along the 20-gauge wire, pushing the coils tightly against each other (whilst holding the 1in/2.5cm tail against the thick wire with the other hand).

3 Continue coiling until you have used all of the 28-gauge wire.
Note: You will have approx ¹⁄₂in (1cm) of 28-gauge wire at either end, which you will not be able to use as it becomes kinked where you have been holding it.

4 Prepare the coils
Trim the wire ends and slide the coils from the 20-gauge wire.

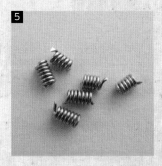

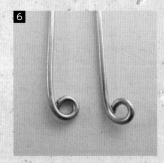

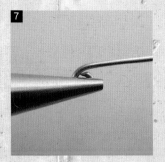

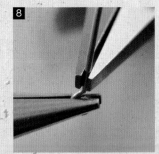

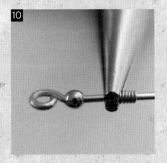

5 Cut the length of coils into sections of approximately seven coils each.
Note: The ends of the wire will stick out slightly, but can be tidied up when you put them on the earwire.

6 Form the earwire
Cut two pieces of 20-gauge wire 2in (5cm) long. Straighten the wire and form a round loop at one end of each piece (see *Simple earwires*, page 20).

7 Grasp the loop with your chain-nose pliers so that the straight wire points the same way as the jaw of the pliers.

8 Grasp the straight wire with the flat-nose pliers, just above the loop and bend upwards by 90°. Repeat with the second earwire.

9 Add beads and coils
Thread one $\frac{1}{16}$in (2mm) bead and one coil onto each earwire. Tip: The coils may be a little tight. If you twist them as you slide them, they will go onto the wire a lot easier.

10 Tuck the ends of the thin wire in by grasping with the chain-nose pliers and twisting the pliers in the same direction as the wire is coiled, crimping the thin wire against the thicker wire.
Note: You should not be able to feel the ends when you run your fingers over the wire. If you can, repeat the action.

11 Shape the earwires
Grasp the earwire just above the coiled wire with the flat-nose pliers and bend 45° in the opposite direction to the opening of the loop.

12 Grasp the straight wire with the thickest part of the round-nose pliers and bend the wire round the jaw, forming a hook.

13 Repeat on other earwire.

14 Final step
Grasp the end of the straight wire with the flat-nose pliers, using the full width of the jaw. Bend upwards by 45°. File or sand the ends so there are no sharp edges. Check that the

wires are straight and in line – if not, give them a squeeze with the nylon-jaw pliers.

Variation
To add an extra detail, you could hammer the curve of the earwire slightly. This also adds strength to the finished piece (see *Hook and 'S' clasp*, page 34).

FIGURE-OF-EIGHT LINKS AND CHAIN

This is a versatile chain, as it can be used with most gauges of wire. You can also use the links as connectors, as a stronger alternative to jump rings.

Materials	Tools
• Approximately 3in (7.5cm) 16-, 18- or 20-gauge soft or half-hard wire per 1in (2.5cm) of chain	• Chain-nose pliers • Round-nose pliers • Flat-nose pliers • Nylon-jaw pliers • Wire cutters • Marker pen • Tape measure

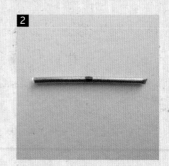

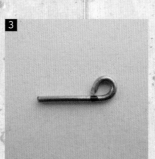

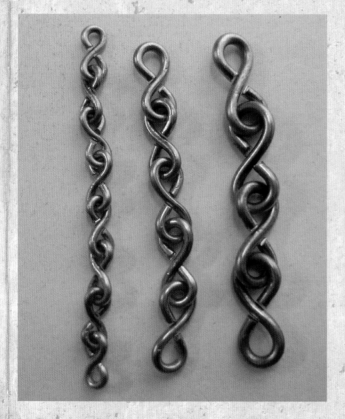

1 Prepare the wire
This is a great way to use up wire off-cuts. First prepare the wire you will be using by cutting it to the correct length and straightening it with the nylon-jaw pliers. Cut it to the following lengths (depending on what gauge you are using):
- ½in (1cm) per link for 20-gauge
- ¾in (2cm) per link for 18-gauge
- 1in (2.5cm) per link for 16-gauge.

Note: The wire length is important, especially when making chain, as it ensures consistent, strong links. If the wire was any shorter, the links would be difficult to form; any longer and it would compromise the strength.

2 Prepare the pliers
Now the wire is ready, you need to ensure that each loop is made on the same point of your round-nose pliers, so they are all the same size. The easiest way to do this is to put a little pen mark on the pliers. First of all, mark the centre point of one of your pieces of wire with a marker pen.

3
Form a loop, so that the end of the wire meets the pen mark. Make a small line on your pliers at the point used to make the loop. Use this point from now on to form all the loops on your chain.

4
The three marks on my pliers are the points I use for 20-gauge, 18-gauge and 16-gauge wire respectively.

5 Form the links

Form a loop (using your pen mark as a guide) at one end of a piece of wire.

6 Grasp this loop in the chain-nose pliers, so that the straight edge points towards the handles of the pliers.

7 Grasp the end with the round-nose pliers, at the point of the pen mark and form a second loop, in the opposite direction to the first.

8 You now have one link.

9 Tidy the link

Snip the very tip of each end of the wire off by holding the cutters at the angle shown. The wire end should sit flush against the central wire. Notice how this opens the links up again.

10 Close the link

Hold one loop in the flat-nose pliers and close the other loop with the chain-nose pliers, taking care that the two ends sit flush against the central wire and are level with each other, forming a straight line.

11 Give the link a squeeze between the nylon-jaw pliers to flatten and harden them.

12 Attach together

Once you have formed your pieces of wire into links, you are ready to form a chain. Hold one loop in the flat-nose pliers, open the other loop with the chain-nose pliers, by twisting the end towards you – do not pull open as this will weaken

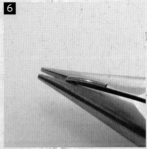

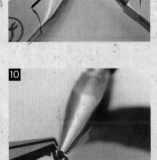

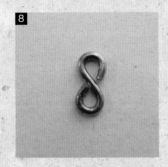

the wire. The link on the left is opened correctly. The one on the right is incorrect.

13 Final step

Thread a link onto the opened one and twist closed.
- Left – 20-gauge wire
- Centre – 18-gauge wire
- Right – 16-gauge wire

Link length:
- 20-gauge = ¼in (5mm)
- 18-gauge = ⅓in (8.5mm)
- 16-gauge = ½in (1cm)

Links per 1in (2.5cm):
- 20-gauge = Six
- 18-gauge = Four
- 16-gauge = Three

Variation – Figure-of-eight tapered link

For the perfect connector for the hook clasp, you can form a tapered figure-of-eight link. To do this, cut 1in (2.5cm) 16-gauge wire and use ¾in (2cm) to form a large loop and ¼in (5mm) for the small loop.

WRAPPED LINK AND CHAIN

These links are an essential technique to have 'up your sleeve'. They are incredibly strong and look very attractive. The links can be used to connect components together or simply used as a chain in their own right.

Materials
- 2½in (6cm) 20-gauge soft or half-hard round wire or 2in (5cm) 24-gauge soft or half-hard round wire per link
- One 3/16in (4mm) round bead (or bead of your choice) per link

Tools
- Chain-nose pliers
- Round-nose pliers
- Flat-nose pliers
- Wire cutters
- Tape measure

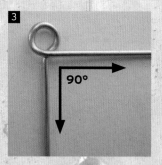

1 Prepare the first loop
For this chain I tend to use 20-gauge wire, for strength and easy manipulation. If, however, your beads have small holes or you would like a more delicate looking chain, you could use 24-gauge wire. Cut a piece of 20-gauge 2½in (6cm) long (2in/5cm for 24-gauge). Measure 1in (2.5cm) from the end and make a 45° bend with the flat-nose pliers.

2 Grasp this bend with the round-nose pliers at a point on the jaws that will give you a loop approximately ⅛in (3mm) in diameter.

3 Wrap the wire all the way round the jaw of the pliers, forming a round loop so that the two straight wires form a 90° angle.

4 Wrap the loop
Grasp the loop with the chain-nose pliers, so that the short straight wire points straight up. Grasp this wire with the flat-nose pliers.

90°

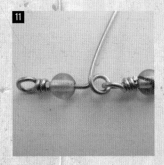

5 Carefully wrap this wire around the long straight wire two-and-a-half times.

6 Make sure that it remains at a 90° angle at all times to keep the wrapping straight.

7 Trim the tail
Cut the tiny tail off, by holding the wire cutters at the angle shown, so that the wire tapers towards the end. This will sit flush against the straight wire.

8 Tuck the end in by pushing it against the straight wire with the chain-nose pliers. You should now have three complete wraps.

9 Form the second loop
Thread a bead onto the wire. Measure ⅛in (3mm) from the end of the bead then grasp with the flat-nose pliers and make a 45° bend.
Tip: You can either do this in the same direction as the first loop, so that both loops face the same way, or at a 90° angle to the first, so that they face opposite directions – this is better for chains, as they tend to hang more freely and not get caught up so easily.

10 Form a wrapped loop by following steps 1–8.

11 Final step
If you are making a chain, form a second link and before wrapping the second loop, thread it onto the loop of the previous link.
Note: You can use any size or type of bead that you like for this chain. The wire measurement given is suitable for up to ⁵⁄₁₆in (6mm) beads. If your beads are larger than this, measure the length of the bead and add 2¼in (5.5cm) for the loops.

12 Wrap the second loop to finish off.
Tip: If you are making a chain, rather than cutting lots of lengths of wire, work with 10in (25cm) or 12in (30cm) at a time. This will save time and also wastage as you will reduce the number of off-cuts.

COILED WIRE CONE

A useful way of hiding multi strand ends, this project teaches you precision placement of wire. It is important there are no spaces between the wire coils as this would compromise the strength and rigidity of the cone.

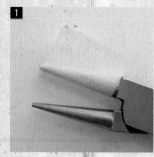

Materials
- 12in (30cm) of 20-gauge half-hard round wire

Tools
- Chain-nose pliers
- Round-nose pliers
- Wire cutters
- Masking/decorators' tape (optional)
- Tape measure

1 Prepare your pliers

The wire cone is shaped by coiling the wire around your round-nose pliers. The grip you have on your pliers is crucial. If it is too loose, the wire will keep turning on itself, resulting in you getting nowhere fast. If it is too tight, you will mark the wire, leaving little divots in the finished cone, making it unattractive. If you struggle to maintain the right grip, try sticking a couple of small pieces of masking tape around one jaw of your pliers. Take care that the tape is smooth and well stuck down on the inside of the jaw to avoid making the situation worse!

2 Begin to form the cone

Cut a piece of 20-gauge wire 12in (30cm) long. Straighten the wire (see *Simple earwires*, page 20). Form a loop around the very tip of the pliers, by grasping the end of the wire and bending it around the jaw of the pliers without the tape. Keep the wire at a 90° angle to the pliers at all times.

3 Continue coiling

Carefully coil around the jaws of the pliers, repositioning the pliers after every turn.

4 Continue until you come to the end of the wire.
Tip: Try to bend the wire around the pliers rather than turning the pliers. This will reduce the pressure you put on the wire with the pliers and thus eliminate marks – it is also better for your hands and wrists!

5 Tidy up the wire ends

Remove the cone from the pliers.

6 Snip the top and bottom loop off (as these will not be perfectly shaped) by holding the wire cutters at an angle as shown.

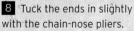

HEADPIN AND BEAD DANGLE

This project shows you how to make your own headpins and how to finish them to create a bead dangle. You can use any size bead you want. To calculate the length of wire required, measure the length of your bead then add ¼ in (5mm) for the head pin end and ½ in (1cm) for the loop.

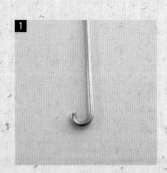

Materials	Tools
• 1in (2.5cm) of 20-gauge soft or half-hard round wire • One ³⁄₁₆ in (4mm) bead	• Chain-nose pliers • Round-nose pliers • Flat-nose pliers • Wire cutters • Tape measure

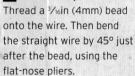

1 Form the headpin end
Cut a piece of 20-gauge wire 1in (2.5cm) long. Form a half loop/semicircle using your round-nose pliers, then snip the end in the same way as for forming a round loop (see *Simple earwires*, page 20).
Tip: In this project I have used 20-gauge wire, but if you have beads with very small holes you could use 24-gauge wire instead, as long as the beads are not too heavy.

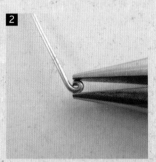

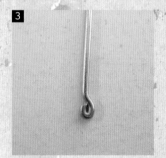

7 Make sure the wire ends are in line with each other so that the cone is straight.

8 Tuck the ends in slightly with the chain-nose pliers.

9 Final step
Don't forget to remove the tape from your pliers and make sure any of the sticky residue is removed.

2 Squeeze the loop closed with the chain-nose pliers as shown.

3 Bend the straight wire upwards by 45º (see *Coiled earwires*, page 22).

4 Form a loop
Thread a ³⁄₁₆ in (4mm) bead onto the wire. Then bend the straight wire by 45º just after the bead, using the flat-nose pliers.

5 Final step
Form a round loop (see *Simple earwires*, page 20).

WRAPPED BRIOLETTE OR DROP

Top-drilled drops and briolettes can add a touch of class to any design. This is a quick and easy method of wrapping them. You can also use this technique to form a stylish bail on top-drilled pendants.

Materials

- 4in (10cm) 20-gauge soft or half-hard round wire
- One top-drilled drop or briolette

Tools

- Chain-nose pliers
- Round-nose pliers
- Flat-nose pliers
- Wire cutters
- Tape measure

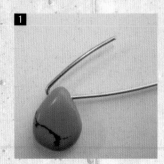

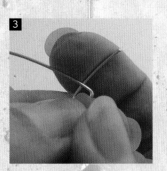

1 Form a triangle
Cut a piece of 20-gauge wire 4in (10cm) long and straighten it. Thread the briolette onto the wire. Measure ½in (1cm) from the end of the wire and make a 135° bend towards the centre of the briolette, using the flat-nose pliers.

2 Measure ¹⁄₁₆in (2mm) from the edge of the briolette and grasp with the flat-nose pliers. Make another 135° bend towards the briolette, forming a triangle.
Tip: You need to be careful whilst forming the triangle, as the top of the briolette is the weakest point of the stone and if you bend the wire too close to the stone you will run the risk of breaking the top.

3 Once you have formed the triangle using the pliers, push the point of this triangle down towards the stone by sliding your finger down the two wires.

4 This will not only make the triangle smaller, but will also make it perfectly even and the point of the triangle will be directly above the centre point of the stone.

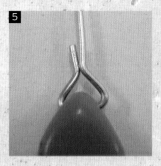
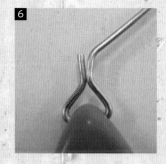
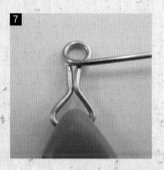

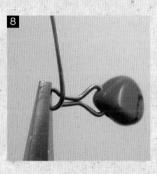

5 Bend the wires

At the point where the two wires cross, grasp with the flat-nose pliers one at a time and bend upwards by 45°, so that they point straight up. Trim the short wire to ⅛in (3mm).

6 Form a loop

Grasp the long wire with the flat-nose pliers, level with the end of the short wire and bend 45° outwards.

7

Grasp just above this bend with the round-nose pliers and form a loop, so that the straight wire forms a 90° angle with the drop.

8 Wrap the loop

In the same way as for the *Wrapped link and chain* (see page 26), wrap the straight wire around the two wires.

9

Keep the wire at a 90° angle at all times until you reach the point where the wires start to separate.
Tip: If your coils are not perfectly straight, use your nylon-jaw pliers to straighten them up, by gently squeezing them together.

10 Final step

Trim and tuck the end in.

BROOCH PIN

This project shows you how to make your own brooch pin. It calls for accurate shaping of the wire, so it is a great way to practise your wire skills.

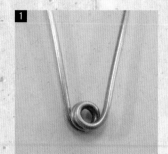

Materials
- 5in (13cm) 18-gauge soft or half-hard round wire

Tools
- Chain-nose pliers
- Round-nose pliers
- Flat-nose pliers
- Nylon-jaw pliers
- Wire cutters
- Rawhide mallet
- Anvil
- File and/or sanding pads
- Tape measure

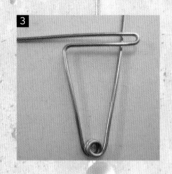

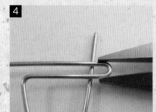

1 Form the spring
Cut a piece of 18-gauge wire 5in (13cm) long and straighten. Measure 1½in (4cm) from one end and grasp with the round-nose pliers. Make a double loop, by wrapping the wire around the jaw of the pliers twice, forming a small spring.

2 Squeeze the spring gently with the nylon-jaw pliers to make sure it is tight and to harden the wire in place. *Note: Do not squeeze too tightly as you will squash the spring, rendering it useless.*

3 Form the catch
Measure 1in (2.5cm) from the spring along the long wire, grasp with the flat-nose pliers and bend 90° towards the pin. Measure ¾in (2cm) from the bend and make a sharp 180° bend.

4 Squeeze this bend closed with the flat-nose pliers.

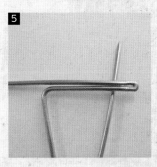  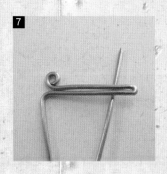 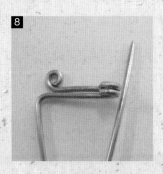

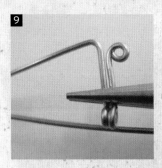   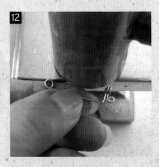

5 Make sure that the two wires run parallel and are touching each other.

6 Form a loop
Bend the short wire by 90° to form a straight line with the back of the pin.

7 Trim to ¼in (5mm) and form a small, round loop (see *Simple earwires*, page 20).

8 Form the catch
Make a very small loop at the end of the double wire, so that it faces away from the pin.

9 Grasp the wires below this loop with the round-nose pliers.

10 Bend the wires round the pliers, to form the catch.

11 Finish the pin
Close the pin and trim this wire level with the end loop. File and/or sand the end of the pin to a smooth point.

12 Final step
Harden the pin by giving it a few taps with the rawhide mallet against the anvil.

HOOK AND 'S' CLASP

A great way to add a unique touch to your handmade jewelry is to make your own clasps from wire. Since you already have this available it saves you money too!

This hook clasp is quick to make and perfect for using with bracelets.

Materials	Tools
• 2in (5cm) 16-gauge round soft or half-hard wire for the hook clasp or 3in (7.5cm) for the 'S' clasp	• Chain-nose pliers • Round-nose pliers • Wire cutters • Hammer • Anvil • Mandrel • Tape measure

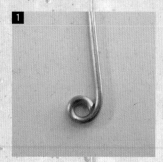

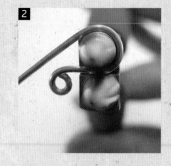

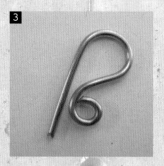

1 Begin to shape the hook clasp
Cut a 2in (5cm) long piece of 16-gauge wire and form a medium-sized round loop in one end (see *Simple earwires*, page 20).

2 Measure ¼in (5mm) from the loop and grasp with the thickest point of your round-nose pliers, bend the straight wire around the jaw of the pliers forming a hook.

3 Notice how it looks like a very thick earwire at this point.

4 Form a second loop
Using the tip of your round-nose pliers, form a small round loop in the end of the wire so that it faces away from the first.

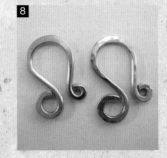

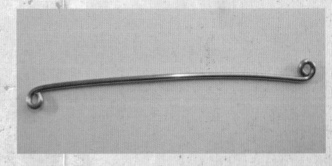

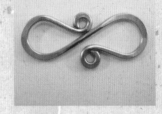

5 Hammer

In order to strengthen the clasp and make it more attractive, you need to flatten it slightly by hammering it. Place the hook on the anvil and carefully hammer the bend on the hook and both loops. You want to hammer it to approximately the same thickness as 20-gauge wire.

6 Use the flat end of the hammer to achieve a smooth finish and the ball end for a textured effect.

Tip: It is better to give the wire lots of little taps and gradually flatten it, rather than one big whack as this gives you a more even finish. Remember over-hammering cannot be undone!

7 The hook on the left has been hammered with the flat end of the hammer and the one on the right with the ball end of the hammer; notice the difference in textures.

8 Final step

Notice how the hammering has forced the shapes to open. Use your chain-nose pliers to close them up.

Variation 'S' clasp

Cut a piece of 16-gauge wire 3in (7.5cm) long. Form small round loops at each end so that they face opposite directions.

Then follow the hook clasp instructions from step 1, forming hooks at both ends and hammering.

SIMPLE T-BAR AND TOGGLE CLASP

A clasp that is very quick to make. It adds great detail to any necklace or bracelet. The bar fits into the ring when turned on its side but can't easily slide out once it has been secured inside the ring as the loops on the ends of the bar lock it into place.

This project is made from two lengths of 16-gauge wire and it teaches you to form a ring and how to hammer sections of the finished clasp.

Once you have mastered this finding, you can make a toggle clasp in any shape you fancy; circles and squares tend to be more secure though than ovals.

Materials
- 7in (18cm) 16-gauge soft or half-hard round wire

Tools
- Chain-nose pliers
- Round-nose pliers
- Flat-nose pliers
- Nylon-jaw pliers
- Wire cutters
- Hammer
- Anvil
- Ring mandrel
- Tape measure

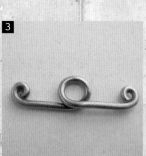

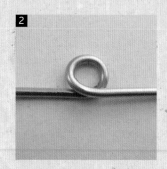

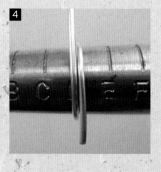

1 Form the bar
Cut a piece of 16-gauge wire 2in (5cm) long and straighten the wire. Form a loop in the centre of the wire by grasping the wire at the centre point with the round-nose pliers and wrapping each end over the top of the jaw.

2 The wires should form a straight line under the loop.

3 Form loops
Form a small round loop at each end of the wire, so that they point the same way as the central loop (see *Simple earwires*, page 20). Set aside.

4 Form the ring
Cut and straighten a piece of 16-gauge wire 5in (13cm) long. Wrap it around your ring mandrel on UK size D (US 2) (or so that you have a ring that is ²⁄₃in (1.7cm) across), by holding ½in (1cm) of the wire in place against the mandrel and wrapping the length of wire around to form a ring.

5 Prepare to form the second loop

Bend both straight wires 90° upwards by grasping with the flat-nose pliers at the point they cross each other. Trim the short wire to ¼in (5mm) from the bend.

6 Form the second loop

Bend the long wire by 45° outwards, level with the top of the short wire.

7 Form a loop using the round-nose pliers. The loop should be the same size as the one on the T-bar. The straight wire should form a 90° angle across the two straight wires.

8 Hold the small loop with your flat-nose pliers and wrap the straight wire around the two parallel wires four or five times, securing them in place. Do not wrap too tightly as they will not sit next to each other.
Tip: Use the chain-nose pliers to help you wrap the wire.

9 Trim

Trim the tail so that the end is tapered, by positioning the wire cutters as shown.

10 Tuck the end in with the chain-nose pliers, so that it does not catch. To avoid marking the wire, straighten the loops using the nylon-jaw pliers.

11 Hammer

Using your anvil and hammer, flatten the top edge of both loops on the ring and all three loops of the T-bar, by positioning the pieces on the edge of the anvil, so that only the bit you want to hammer is on the flat surface.
Tip: Give the pieces lots of little taps, working your way round the loops and ring evenly. Remember one or two big whacks may irreparably spoil your work. You want to achieve the same thickness as 20-gauge wire.

12 Notice how the bar is no longer straight and the loops have opened.

13 Final step

Close the loops but leave the bar this shape, ensuring it locks into place in the ring.

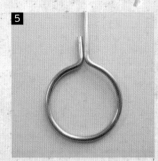

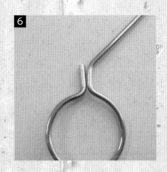

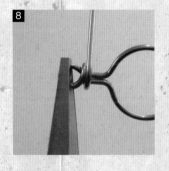

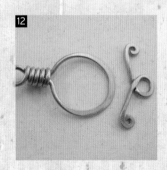

COILED T-BAR AND TOGGLE CLASP

A more ornate version of the simple toggle clasp, this variation is incredibly strong and is attractive enough to use as the focal point on a simple chain necklace.

Materials
- 11in (28cm) 16-gauge soft or half-hard round wire
- 56in (1.42m) 24-gauge soft or half-hard round wire

Tools
- Chain-nose pliers
- Round-nose pliers
- Flat-nose pliers
- Nylon-jaw pliers
- Wire cutters
- Ring mandrel
- Sanding pads
- Tape measure

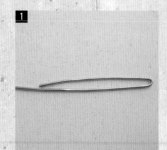

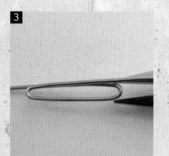
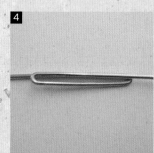

1 Begin to form the T-bar
Cut a piece of 16-gauge wire 5in (13cm) long and straighten. Measure 2in (5cm) from one end and, grasping with the flat-nose pliers, make a 180° bend.

2 Measure 1 1/8in (2.8cm) from the bend along the long wire. Grasp with the flat-nose pliers and make another 180° bend, so that the two wires cross at the top. The bottom wire is 1in (2.5cm) long.

3 Grasp one bend in the flat-nose pliers and carefully squeeze together until the bar is 1/8in (3mm) wide.

4 Take care that your pliers do not slip as this will mark the wire. If this does happen, sand any marks out by starting with the roughest grit and working down to the smoothest.

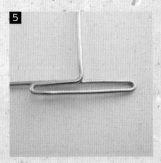

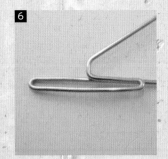

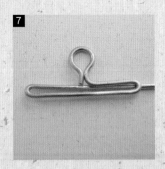

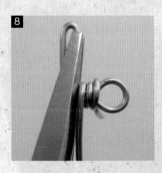

5 Form the loop

Grasp one of the straight top wires with the flat-nose pliers in the centre of the bar and bend upwards by 90°.
Note: This upwards pointing wire will not be quite central to the bar.

6 Measure 1/8in (3mm) up from the bend and make a 45° bend to the right.

7 Grasp this bend with the round-nose pliers and form a medium loop, then bend the wire downwards by 90° and trim to 1/8in (3mm).

8 Grasp the bar in the flat-nose pliers as shown and wrap the loop closed three times. Trim and tuck the end in.

9 Check all is straight and adjust with the nylon-jaw pliers if necessary. Notice how the bar looks a little bit like a coat hanger at this point!

10 Bind

Cut a piece of 24-gauge wire 23in (58.5cm) long and attach it to one end of the bar by coiling twice. Bind the two wires together until you reach the centre (approximately 18 times). Ensure the binding is neat and straight by keeping the 24-gauge wire at a 90° angle to the 16-gauge wire at all times.

11 Coil the bottom wire eight times, until you are past the loop. Then bind the other side, leaving room to coil twice once you reach the other end, to secure the wire and stop your binding from slipping off the end of the bar. Trim and tuck the end in.

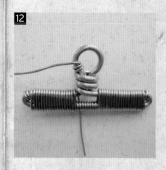

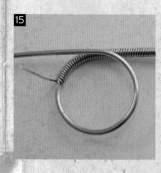

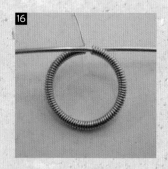

12 Coil the loop

You should have at least 6in (15cm) of 24-gauge wire left over from binding the bar. If you have less than 6in (15cm) at this point, simply cut a new piece. Attach the 24-gauge to the loop, by coiling three times, leaving a 1in (2.5cm) tail (to hold onto).

13 Continue coiling until you reach the other side of the loop, trim the ends inside the ring and tuck in so that they are hidden.

14 Form the ring

The ring is constructed in much the same way as the bar. Cut a piece of 16-gauge wire 6in (15cm) long and straighten. Wrap the centre of the wire once around the ring mandrel on UK size L (US size 5½).

15 Coil

Cut a piece of 24-gauge wire 33in (84cm) long. Attach it to one of the straight wires from the ring, by coiling three times and leaving a 1in (2.5cm) tail. Continue coiling until you have covered 2⅛in (5.4cm).

16 Slide the coils round the ring taking care not to distort the shape.

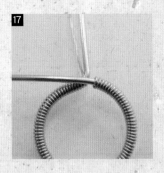 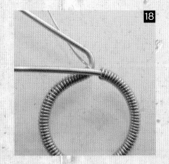 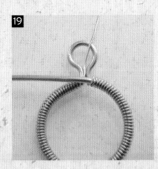

17 Form the loop
Bend one straight wire
upwards by 90°.

18 Measure ⅛ in (3mm)
up from this bend and bend
outwards by 45°.

19 Form a loop (the same
size as the loop on the T-bar)
and then bend the wire 90°
downwards. Trim the wire
level with the top of the ring.

20 Grasp the ring with the
nylon-jaw pliers and wrap
the straight wire around the
two parallel 16-gauge wires
and the 24-gauge wire three
times. Trim and then tuck
the end in.

21 Final step
With the 24-gauge wire, coil
the loop all the way round,
then trim and tuck the end in.

EASY PROJECTS

The projects in this section will allow you to practise
your newly learned skills from the first section and also
offers some more skills and techniques for you to learn,
including weaving and making spirals.

This section covers easy projects, but the designs
are challenging enough for even the most
advanced wireworker to enjoy.

Below is a list of the projects in this section and the skills and techniques they cover:

Dragon's tear
- Making wrapped briolette
  or drop
- Making earwires

Nebula
- Making wrapped link chain
- Making coiled wire cones
- Making a simple T-bar and
  toggle clasp

Cascade
- Making a wrapped link
  chain
- Making coiled wire cones
- Making a coiled toggle
  clasp
- Making a wrapped
  briolette or drop

Butterfly wing
- Forming a wire frame
  using open spirals
- Embellishing with thin
  wire
- Securely attaching beads
  to the frame

Vortex
- Forming a ring shank
- Enlarging a bead hole
- Wrapping a bead to form
  a focal point

Orbital
- Weaving 2 straight wires
  to form a frame
- Forming a single, closed
  spiral
- Forming a woven bail

DRAGON'S TEAR
BRIOLETTE EARRINGS

This is the first of three projects that show
you some suggested uses for the findings in
the first section of the book.

These earrings will complement any piece of jewelry and
are easy to co-ordinate with any outfit as well as being quick
and fun to make with striking results.

Materials (for one pair)
- 16in (40cm) 20-gauge
  half-hard round wire
- 2 briolettes or drops
- Two $3/16$in (4mm) beads

Tools
- Chain-nose pliers
- Round-nose pliers
- Flat-nose pliers
- Nylon-jaw pliers
- Wire cutters
- Tape measure

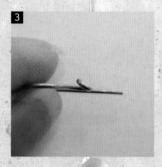

1 Preparation
Make one pair of simple earwires and two wrapped briolettes, following the instructions in the 'Findings and Basic Techniques' section (see pages 20 and 30).

2 Connect findings to a wrapped link
Form a wrapped link with a bead of your choice. Once you have formed the second loop, thread the briolette onto the wire and then wrap the loop.

3 Attach the earwire
Open the loop on the earwire by twisting to one side. Thread the earring on (ensuring it is facing the correct way).

4 Final step
Twist the earwire loop closed again with the chain-nose pliers. Repeat the process with the second earring.

Variation

You can use any combination
of drops and beads you like
– the length of the earring
will depend on the size of
the beads you choose. The
example here has a 2in (5cm)
drop, using a $3/16$in (4mm)
bead and a $3/4$in (2cm) drop.

NEBULA
MULTI-STRAND BRACELET

This bracelet uses many of the components taught
in the previous section, combining them to form a simple
yet striking design, which can be greatly altered by
your choice of beads.

*This bracelet is 7¹⁄₂in (19cm) long. To make it larger or smaller
simply increase or decrease the number of links in the chains.*

Materials
- 40in (1.02m) 24-gauge
  soft or half-hard round wire
- 32in (81cm) 20-gauge
  soft or half-hard round wire
- 7in (18cm) 16-gauge soft
  or half-hard round wire
- 54 x semi-precious chips
  and eight ³⁄₁₆ in (4mm)
  round beads

Tools
- Chain-nose pliers
- Round-nose pliers
- Flat-nose pliers
- Nylon-jaw pliers
- Wire cutters
- Hammer
- Anvil
- Ring mandrel
- Tape measure

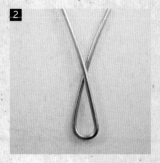

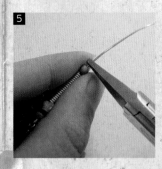

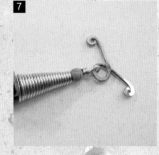

1 Preparation

Make the following items from the 'Findings and Basic Techniques' section (see pages 26–29 and 36):

- Two coiled wire cones
- One simple T-bar and toggle clasp
- Three 4in (10cm) lengths of wrapped chain.

If you are using $3/16$in (4mm) beads, there will be approximately 10 links per chain; for chips there will be approximately eight to nine links per chain.

I have used 24-gauge wire to make the chain for this bracelet. As there are three lengths, strength is not so much of an issue. It also gives the chain a more delicate look. You can use 20-gauge wire if you prefer.

2 Connect the pieces

Cut a piece of 20-gauge wire 4in (10cm) long. Measure 1in (2.5cm) from one end, grasp with the round-nose pliers and form a medium-sized loop.

3

Thread the three lengths of chain onto the loop. Bend the long wire upwards by 45° and the short wire downwards by 45° forming a 90° angle between the two wires.

4

Grasp the loop with the chain-nose pliers and wrap the short wire around the long wire twice, trim the tail and tuck the end in.

5 Attach the clasp

Thread a wire cone and a $3/16$in (4mm) bead onto the straight wire, holding these in place between the thumb and forefinger of your less dominant hand. Grasp just above the bead with your flat-nose pliers and bend by 45°.

6

Form a round loop, thread the ring onto the loop and wrap three times. Trim the tail and tuck the end in (see *Wrapped link and chain*, page 26). As you coil, you will notice that this action pushes the bead and cone tightly together, increasing the strength of the cone.

7

Follow steps 2–6 on the other end of the bracelet, attaching the T-bar and ensuring all three chains are parallel when attached.

8 Final step

Once you have secured your cones, gently squeeze the three chains together, so that they hang nicely.

Variation

The style of this bracelet can be greatly affected by the type of beads you choose; small, round beads give it a very sleek look, while semi-precious chips give a strong ethnic feel. For this variation you will need 32 x $^3/_{16}$in (4mm) round beads, instead of the beads detailed in the materials list.

CASCADE
LARIAT NECKLACE

You know the saying 'practice makes perfect'? Well, it applies as much to wirework as anything else and this necklace is the ideal project for getting to grips with the basic techniques, due to its repetitive construction.

This is a time-consuming design to make, because of the length of the necklace (27in/68.5cm in total) and the number of components, but it's well worth the effort.

Materials

- Approx. 150in (3.8m) 20-gauge soft or half-hard round wire
- 33in (84cm) 24-gauge soft or half-hard wire
- 6in (15cm) 16-gauge soft or half-hard wire
- 48 x $^3/_{16}$in (4mm) round beads (or beads of your choice)
- Three to six briolette or drops

Tools

- Chain-nose pliers
- Round-nose pliers
- Flat-nose pliers
- Nylon-jaw pliers
- Wire cutters
- Ring mandrel
- Tape measure

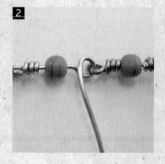
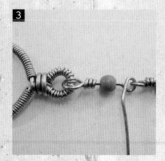

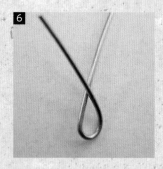

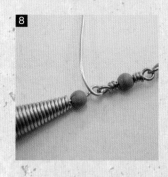

1 Preparation

Since this necklace is made using the components from the first section, the first thing to do is to prepare all of these items so that they are ready to connect together. Make the following items using the instructions in the 'Findings and Basic Techniques' section (see pages 20–41):

- One coiled ring (from Coiled T-bar and Toggle Clasp)
- One wire cone
- Three or six wrapped briolettes
- One wrapped chain 20½in (52cm) long (approximately 38 links)
- One wrapped chain four links long
- One wrapped chain two links long.

2 If you are finding it too hard to manage the long length of chain, you might find it easier to make two sections of chain 10¼in (26cm) long, joined together.

3 Connect the ring

Attach the coiled ring to one end of the chain using a wrapped link (see pages 26-7), remembering to attach the chain to one end and the ring to the other end before coiling! Make the loop for the coiled ring larger than normal to accommodate the 16-gauge wire.

4 Prepare the tassels

Form a wrapped link, attaching one or two wrapped briolettes (depending on your design). Remember if you are attaching two, you need to make the loop slightly larger so that they hang freely.

5 Make two more tassels in the same way, one with the two-link chain and the other with the four-link chain.

6 Attach the tassels to the chain

Cut a piece of 20-gauge wire 4in (10cm) long. Measure 1in (2.5cm) from one end and, grasping with the round-nose pliers, wrap the 1in (2.5cm) tail around the jaws forming a loop.

7 Thread the tassels onto the wire, shortest to longest, making sure they all face the same way. Bend the long wire upwards by 45° and the short wire downwards by 45° forming a 90° angle.

To close the loop, wrap the short wire around the long wire twice, trim and tuck the end in, leaving the vertical wire.

8 Final step

Thread the open end of the cone, then the 3/16in (4mm) bead onto the straight wire. Form a loop. Attach the unfinished end of the chain onto the open loop and wrap the loop closed.

Variation
You can experiment with
different shapes and the
colours of beads to create
a variety of effects.

BUTTERFLY WING
DOUBLE SPIRAL EARRINGS

A deceptively simple design, which can be dressed up or down with your choice of beads and wire. Use copper and round stone beads for a more casual look, or silver and faceted rondelles to create a chic pair of earrings.

Note: These earrings have a 1¼in (3cm) drop (including the coiled earwire) and the wirework is ¾in (2cm) long and ½in (1cm) wide. The metal beads must have a hole that is large enough for the 28-gauge wire to pass through twice.

Materials
- One pair of earwires of your choice (pages 20–23)
- 6in (15cm) 18-gauge soft or half-hard round wire
- 22in (56cm) 28-gauge soft or half-hard round wire
- Two ³/₁₆in (4mm) round or rondelle stone beads
- Two ⅛in (3mm) round metal beads
- Two ³/₃₂in (2.5mm) round metal beads
- Two ¹/₁₆in (2mm) round metal beads

Tools
- Chain-nose pliers
- Round-nose pliers
- Flat-nose pliers
- Nylon-jaw pliers
- Wire cutters
- Marker pen
- Tape measure/ruler

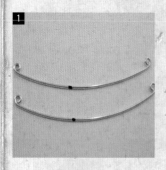   

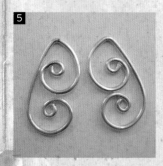 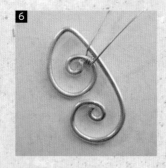 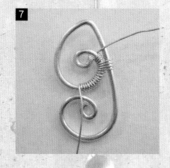 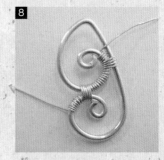

1 Preparing the frame wire
Cut two pieces of 18-gauge wire 3in (7.5cm) long. Measure 1¼in (3cm) from one end and mark with a marker pen on both pieces of wire. Form a round loop at both ends of each piece, facing the same direction.

2 Form open spirals
Grasp one of the loops with the chain-nose pliers.

3 Hold the other end of the wire between thumb and forefinger then carefully turn both the pliers and your hand, allowing the pliers to determine the distance between the loop and wire. Form an open spiral, for three-quarters of a turn.

4 Repeat the process with the second wire.
Note: With each wire, the second spiral will be slightly harder to form due to the wire being shorter and also the work hardening from forming the first spiral.

5 Finish the frame
Grasp the frame with the flat-nose pliers where your pen mark is and bend inwards until the top spiral touches the straight wire. Clean the pen marks off with a soft cloth. Squeeze between the nylon-jaw pliers to flatten out the frame and harden the wire into position. Repeat with the second wire.
Tip: You may need to slightly adjust the bottom spirals, so that the frame sits flat.

6 Attach a thin wire
Cut a piece of 28-gauge wire 11in (28cm) long. Leaving a 1in (2.5cm) tail (to hold onto), attach the wire to the frame, just below the top loop, by coiling it three times around the frame wire.

7 Bind the spiral to the straight wire four times keeping the 28-gauge wire at a 90° angle to the frame wire at all times to ensure the binding is straight. Continue coiling 11 times. Slide the coils and binding along the frame wire with your thumbnail, to keep it tight and neat.

8 Close the frame
Bind the top spiral to the bottom spiral four to five times, securing the frame closed. Then coil the lower spiral seven times; this is very important as it marks the space for the stone bead, which is attached last.

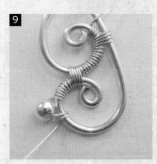

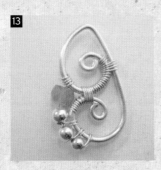

Variations

Hammer the frames slightly to flatten before attaching the 28-gauge wire. Follow the instructions to step 5, coil four times and trim the wire. This can be oxidized (see 'Tools and Materials', page 17) to highlight the detail.

9 Attach a bead

Thread a ⅛in (3mm) metal bead onto the 28-gauge wire. Hold the bead in place between thumb and forefinger on the outer edge of the frame wire, take the 28-gauge wire round the frame wire and coil once, pulling it tightly to secure. The bead should still be able to move around on the frame.

10 Attach the ³⁄₃₂in (2.5mm) and ¹⁄₁₆in (2mm) beads in the same way.

11 Secure the beads

Thread the 28-gauge wire back through all three beads. You will probably need to do this one at a time, so be very careful not to kink the wire. Pull very tightly, so that the three beads sit closely together. They should no longer be able to move around the frame.

12 Add the final bead

Thread the ³⁄₁₆in (4mm) bead onto the wire and coil the top spiral four times, securing it in place.

13 Trim the end of the wire and the 1in (2.5cm) tail on the inside of the frame and tuck the ends in. Squeeze the frame between the nylon-jaw pliers to flatten the binding.

14 Final step

Repeat steps 6–13 on the other frame so that you have a matching pair. Attach the earwires, making sure that the earrings face in opposite directions.

VORTEX
WRAPPED RING

This is such a quick ring to make - you can have one to match every outfit in every colour! Constructed from a single length of wire, the wrapping around the stone bead ensures a solid and hard-wearing design.

Note: This lesson will give you a finished ring UK size I (US size 4¼). The wire length given is suitable for sizes up to UK size K (US size 5), any larger, add approximately 1in (2.5cm) per size increase.

Materials
- 20in (50cm) 20-gauge soft round wire
- One ⁵/₁₆in (6mm) bead (preferably with a ¹/₃₂in/ 1mm hole or larger)

Tools
- Chain-nose pliers
- Flat-nose pliers
- Nylon-jaw pliers
- Wire cutters
- Bead reamer/round needle file (optional – if bead holes require enlarging)
- Ring mandrel
- Tape measure

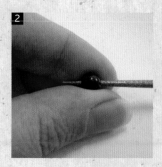
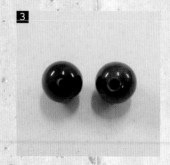

1 Check the size of your bead hole

The first thing to do is check that two pieces of 20-gauge wire can fit through the hole of the bead.

2 If not, carefully enlarge the hole using a bead reamer or round needle file. In order to avoid chipping or damaging your bead, it is better to hold the bead stationary and rotate the file or reamer in the hole – don't apply too much pressure as the bead may crack. Remember to enlarge both ends of the hole.

3 The bead on the right has the correct size hole.

4 Form the shank

Once your bead is ready, begin to make the ring. Take the piece of 20in (50cm) long 20-gauge wire and straighten. Wrap the centre of the wire around the ring mandrel on UK size M (US size 6). Then wrap once either side, giving three wraps in total.

Tip: Take care that the wires do not cross and that they lie neatly next to each other. If you are using a tapered mandrel, remove the shank from the mandrel and turn it around, to even the wraps and the size.

Note: The finished ring will be four UK sizes smaller than the working size, due to the wrapping, so your finished size for this ring will be UK size I (US size 4¹/₄).

5 Thread the bead onto the ring

Lift the two wire ends, so that they meet above the mandrel, thread the bead onto both wires, making sure that the wires do not cross over each other inside the bead. Grasp each wire with the flat-nose and chain-nose pliers and carefully pull the wires through.

6 Tighten each side while holding the bead in place, ensuring it sits on top of the two wires of the shank and that it is straight.

7 Begin to wrap the bead

In order to ensure the wrapping around the bead is central to the ring, bend both wires that feed into the bead from the shank 45° downwards, using the flat-nose pliers.

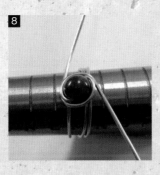

8 Still working on the mandrel, form a circle round the bead, by bending each straight wire around the bead for half a turn. Notice how this pulls the shank wires out of line and turns the bead slightly; don't worry, this can be straightened up later.

9 Continue wrapping the bead
Wrap the bead five times in total, working both wires at the same time to ensure an even wrap. Keep a consistent tension on the wires and make sure that each wrap sits beneath the previous one.

10 Coil the shank
Remove the ring from the mandrel. Hold the bead and wrapping in place between the thumb and forefinger of your less dominant hand, then wrap each side of the shank twice, taking care to keep the wrapping straight. This will lock everything securely in place.
Tip: Use your chain-nose pliers to help pull the wire around the shank.

11 Continue coiling until you have nine wraps each side of the shank. It is important the shank wires sit neatly next to each other and do not become bunched up, so do not pull too tightly. The two wires from the shank should also remain underneath the bead. Notice that the bead and wrapping are not quite straight yet.

12 Trim the wire tails on the inside of the shank, next sand the ends to ensure there are no sharp edges and tuck the ends in with chain-nose pliers.

13 Final step
All you need to do now is straighten the bead and wrapping. Put the ring onto the mandrel, then grasp the wrapping with the nylon-jaw pliers and twist slightly towards the shank to straighten. Repeat on the opposite side.

ORBITAL
WOVEN ROUND PENDANT

This is the first project in the book to look at wire weaving.
It teaches you how to make a frame around a bead.
The weaving not only ensures a solid structure but also
adds wonderfully ornate detail. This reversible pendant
is complimented with a closed spiral on either side and
is ideal for people with fiddly fingers, as the bead is able
to rotate in its setting!

*Note: You can use half-hard wire instead but you will need to
follow steps 10 and 11.*

Materials
- 12$\frac{1}{2}$in (31cm) 18-gauge soft round wire
- 60in (152cm) 28-gauge soft round wire
- One $^9/_{16}$in (1.4cm) round bead

Tools
- Chain-nose pliers
- Round-nose pliers
- Flat-nose pliers
- Nylon-jaw pliers
- Wire cutters
- Masking tape
- Ring mandrel (optional, only required if using half-hard wire)
- Pin/needle
- Tape measure/ruler

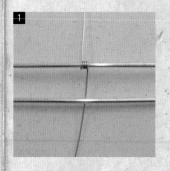
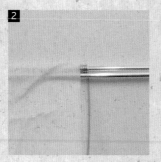
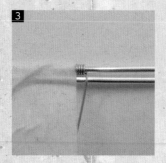
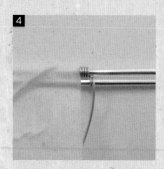

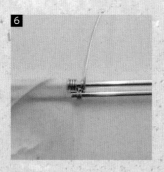
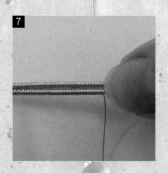
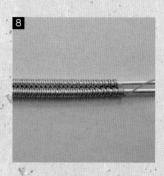

1 Prepare the frame wires

Cut two pieces of 18-gauge wire 6¼in (15.5cm) long and straighten. Cut one piece of 28-gauge wire 30in (76cm) long. Measure 2¼in (5.5cm) along one of the pieces of 18-gauge wire and attach the 28-gauge wire by coiling three times, leaving a 1in (2.5cm) tail (use this to hold the wire in place). Ensure that the coils are tight by sliding them along the thick wire with your thumbnail.

2 Prepare to weave

The two structure wires are secured together with the weaving. To allow room for the 28-gauge wire to pass between them, you need to ensure there is at least a ¹⁄₃₂in (1mm) gap. The easiest way to do this is to tape the 18-gauge wires in place with masking tape. Measure 2¼in (5.5cm) along the wires and attach the tape, securing the 1in (2.5cm) tail of 28-gauge wire in place too, pushing the coils against the tape and securing them in place.

3 Begin to weave

Now everything is secured in place, you are ready to weave. Take the 28-gauge wire under the top structure wire and over the bottom one.

4 Coil the bottom wire once, pulling tightly, securing the first weave in place.
Tip: When weaving, take great care not to allow loops to form in your weaving wire, as when you pull the wire, a loop becomes a kink and this will weaken the wire and cause it to snap.

5 Take the wire back

Bring the 28-gauge wire under the bottom wire and over the top structure wire.

6 Coil the top wire once, pulling it tightly. Keep sliding the weave along the structure wire with your thumbnail, so it sits neatly against the tape.

7 Continue

Keep weaving under, over, coil once, and pushing the weave tightly together until you have covered 1¾in (4.5cm) of the structure wires.

8 Coil three times on the bottom wire to secure the 28-gauge wire and carefully remove the tape.
Tip: Try to avoid running the 28-gauge wire through your fingers as this makes it springy and more liable to kinking and snapping. Instead try to hold the tip of the wire, treating it as a needle.

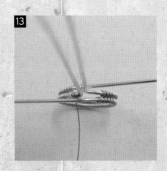

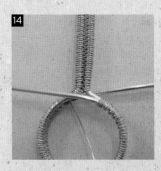

9 Shape the frame

Check that the weaving is central to the structure wires and adjust if necessary, by sliding the weaving along the wires. You should have 2¼in (5.5cm) of wire on either side of the 1¾in (4.5cm) section of weaving. Trim the tails on the inside of the frame and tuck the ends in. If you have used soft wire, you can wrap the frame directly around the centre of the bead. Ensure the wires interlock at the top of the frame.

10 If you have used half-hard wire, it will be too stiff, so use the ring mandrel and wrap the woven frame around UK size F (US size 3), to ensure that you have a true circle.

11 Once you have wrapped the wire around the mandrel, slide your thumb down the structure wires to the point where they cross against the mandrel, and push them into place. Ensure the wires interlock at the top of the frame.

12 Shape the bail

Now that the frame is shaped, we need to prepare the bail wires ready for weaving. Using the flat-nose pliers, bend the two central structure wires upwards by 90° at the point where they cross each other. The two wires should be pointing straight up and be sitting next to each other.

13 Weave the bail

Cut a piece of 28-gauge wire 30in (76cm) long. Attach it to the left bail wire, by coiling four to six times just below the bend, leaving an 8in (20cm) tail (this will be used later to attach the bead and secure the bail closed).

14 Weave in the same way as you did on the frame – under, over, coil once – until you have covered 1in (2.5cm). Keep pushing the weave tightly together.

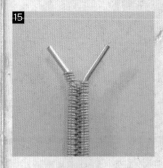

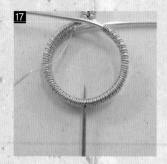

15 Secure the weaving
Coil the nearest thick wire three times to secure, then trim and tuck the end in on the inside of the frame. Trim both the 18-gauge bail wires to ¼in (5mm) and bend outwards by 45°.

16 Form a small round loop at the end of both wires. Trim the two straight wires on the frame to 1in (2.5cm) from the bail.

17 Attach the bead
In order to attach the bead, the 28-gauge wire has to pass through the weaving at the bottom of the frame. To make room for this, push a pin or needle into the frame directly below the bail.

18 Thread the bead onto the 28-gauge wire. Take the wire through the weaving (using the gap you created with the pin), round the frame and back through the bead, pulling tightly. Coil the opposite side of the frame three times to secure.

19 Form two spirals
Make a round loop at the end of both straight wires. Once the loop is closed, keep turning to start the spiral.

20 Grasp the loop with the flat-nose pliers and turn the pliers so the wire begins to form a circle around the loop. Build this circle up gradually, by repositioning the pliers, until you have a full rotation, completing the spiral.

21 Check the spiral is central to the bail and push it against the stone with your fingers or nylon-jaw pliers. Repeat on the other side.

22 Shape the bail
Grasp the bail wires at their base with the nylon-jaw pliers and bend backwards by 45°.

Variation

Instead of two small loops (see step 16), trim the bail wires to 1in (2.5cm) after weaving and form two closed spirals. Push these spirals against the bail, adding extra detail to the side view of the pendant.

23 Measure ½in (1cm) along the bail wires and bend over your round-nose pliers (do not grasp with the pliers as you will mark the wire). Then bend the loops upwards by 45°.

24 Close the bail
Holding the bail closed between thumb and forefinger of your less dominant hand, bind the bail closed by taking the 28-gauge wire under the frame and round one of the loops. (See circled area.) Repeat this twice each side, pulling tightly to lock the wires in place.

25 Coil one of the loops three times to secure, trim and tuck the end in. The binding should be invisible now.

26 Final step
Turn the loops so that they sit on top of the frame, using the flat-nose pliers.

INTERMEDIATE PROJECTS

You should now have quite an array of skills and techniques
under your belt, from hammering to weaving.

This section takes those a step further.

Below is a list of the projects in this section and the skills and techniques they cover:

Mermaid's purse
- Forming a matching pair of frames
- Hammering
- Attaching a briolette

Eastern charm
- Developing a design (*Mermaid's purse* hammered earrings)
- Attaching chain and bead dangles to a frame wire

Crescent
- Forming a shaped ring shank
- Securing beads in the open space

Daisy
- Forming post earrings
- Forming a setting for a bead

Fern frond
- Forming multiple structure wires and secure together
- Attaching bead and briolette decoration to the structure wires
- Forming a 'bird's nest setting'

Boudica
- Forming a double spiral frame with a single wire
- Attaching wire spiral detail for decoration and strength
- Connecting multiple links
- Hammering

Ammonite
- Weaving on a curve

MERMAID'S PURSE
HAMMERED EARRINGS

Make a pair of droplet-style earrings. A contrast of textures is created by hammering the frame wire, then wrapping a section of that frame with 28-gauge wire. This project also teaches you how to make a wrapped connector using 28-gauge wire – a very useful technique for connecting frame wires together.

The briolette is attached inside the frame and is able to swivel in its setting, adding movement to the design.

Materials (for one pair)
- 8in (20cm) 18-gauge half-hard round wire
- 30in (76cm) 28-gauge soft or half-hard round wire
- Two briolettes $1/2$–$3/4$in (1–2cm)
- One pair of coiled earwires

Tools
- Chain-nose pliers
- Round-nose pliers
- Nylon-jaw pliers
- Wire cutters
- Hammer
- Anvil
- Ring mandrel
- $1/8$in (3mm) diameter mandrel (kebab stick, knitting needle, wooden dowel, etc)
- Tape measure/ruler

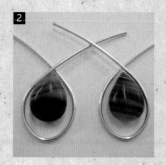

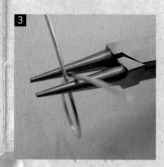

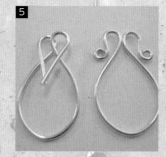

1 Prepare the frame wires
Cut two pieces of 18-gauge wire 4in (10cm) long. Wrap the centre of the wire around the mandrel at UK size C (US size 1¾) and form a loop approx ¾in (2cm) high, by sliding your thumb down the straight wires and pushing the crossover against the mandrel.

2 The two straight wires should measure 1in (2.5cm) each. Check your briolettes fit inside the loops and that both frames are identical.
Note: You are only using the mandrel to obtain a nice smooth curve on the bottom of the loop – the sides should remain straight.

3 Shape the frames
Grasp the frame with the centre point of the round-nose pliers, at the point where the wires cross.

4 Bend the wire outwards and round the jaw, forming it into two loops. Be sure to reposition the pliers, so that both loops are formed on the same point of the jaws.

5 Trim the straight wires to ¼in (5mm) from where they cross the main frame and form round loops. Flatten with the nylon-jaw pliers.

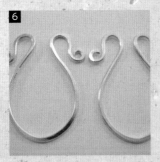
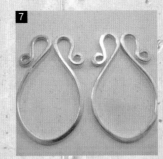

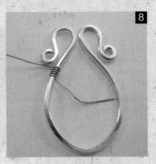
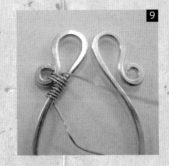
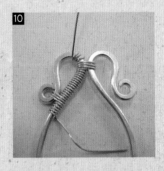

6 Hammer
Carefully flatten the frames to the same thickness as 20-gauge (0.8mm) wire using the hammer and anvil. Notice how this makes the loops open and the frame separate slightly.

7 Close the loops again and check that both frames are the same.

8 Attach a thin wire
Cut a piece of 28-gauge wire 15in (38cm) long. Attach it to the left of the frame, just below the small loop, by coiling five times, leaving a 1in (2.5cm) tail.

9 Bind the loop to the frame three times to secure in place. Make sure that each bind is straight and tight.

10 Coil the frame 15 times, then bind the two top loops together three times and coil the left side of the frame three times. Keep the binding and coiling tightly together, by sliding it along the frame wire with your thumbnail. Always keep the coiling wire at a 90° angle to the frame wire to ensure it is positioned correctly.

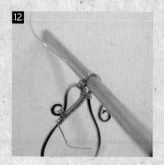

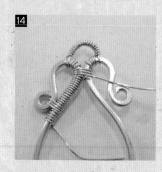

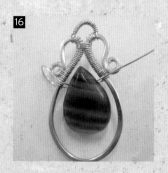

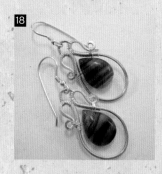

11 Form the wrapped connector

To hang the earring, you need to form a connector between the two top loops. To do this, hold your ⅛in (3mm) mandrel in place, so it sits between the two top loops. Take the thin wire over the top of the mandrel, through the right hand loop and back over the top of the mandrel and through the left loop.

12

Coil the two pieces of 28-gauge wire together. Tip: Make the first couple of coils with the mandrel in place, to make sure the connector keeps its shape.

13

Take care that your wire is placed accurately when coiling. Repositioning is difficult as the two thin wires are not rigid enough to push against.

14 Coil the frame

Coil the top loop three times. Then take the wire behind the binding and round the frame below it.

15

Mirror the left side by coiling 15 times, binding the loop to the frame three times, and then coil the frame once. Trim the 1in (2.5cm) tail on the inside of the frame and tuck in.

16 Attach the briolette

Thread the briolette onto the 28-gauge wire. Take the wire round the frame, just below the binding on the left and back through the briolette.

17

Pull tightly so that the wire locks into place between the coiling. Coil the frame four times to secure and trim.

18 Final step

Repeat on the other frame. Squeeze the binding with the nylon-jaw pliers to flatten. Attach the coiled earwires.

Variations
Using different-sized briolettes
will change the look of the
earrings dramatically, as
does using faceted stones.

EASTERN CHARM
DANGLE EARRINGS

It is easy to transform a design by dressing it up or down. This project shows you how to develop the *Mermaid's purse* earrings (see page 73) into something fit for a Bollywood film set! Instead of hammering the frame, it is coiled with 28-gauge wire for a more ornate look. Chain and bead dangles are added to give movement and colour.

These earrings have a 2¼in (5.5cm) drop including the earwire. The actual earring is 1²/₃in (4.2cm) long by ²/₃in (1.7cm) wide.

Materials (for one pair)
- 8in (20cm) 18-gauge half-hard round wire
- 9in (23cm) 24-gauge soft or half-hard round wire
- 76in (1.93m) 28-gauge soft or half-hard round wire
- 14 x ³/₁₆in (4mm) round beads
- Two briolettes ½–³/₄in (1–2cm)
- 2in (5cm) chain (bought or handmade)
- One pair of coiled earwires

Tools
- Chain-nose pliers
- Flat-nose pliers
- Round-nose pliers
- Nylon-jaw pliers
- Wire cutters
- Ring mandrel
- ⅛in (3mm) diameter mandrel (kebab stick, knitting needle, wooden dowel, etc)
- Tape measure/ruler

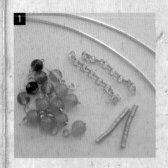

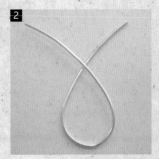

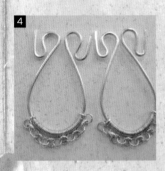

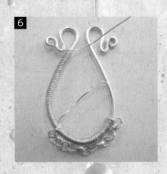

1 Preparation

The first thing to do is get all of the components ready for the earrings. Prepare the following items (see pages 20–41):

- 14 bead dangles, using 24-gauge wire and ³/₁₆in (4mm) beads
- Two 1in (2.5cm) lengths of chain, or you can use bought chain if you prefer. Make sure you have an odd number of links on both pieces, to give a central point to attach the dangle
- Two ½in (1cm) lengths of coiled 28-gauge wire, wrapped around the 18-gauge wire (approx. 8in/20cm of 28-gauge is required per ½in/1cm of coiling)
- Two 4in (10cm) lengths of 18-gauge wire.

2 Shape the frames

Following the instructions for the *Mermaid's purse* earrings step 1 (see page 73), forming a loop in the centre of both 18-gauge wires.

3 Slide the ½in (1cm) coils onto each frame, and then thread the loop from each end of the chain onto the frame, either side of the coils. Make sure that the chain is straight and not twisted.

Tip: Form both earrings at the same time to ensure they are identical.

4 Finish shaping the frames

Now that the coils and chain are in place on the frames the shaping can be finished. Follow the instructions for the *Mermaid's purse* earrings steps 3–5 to form the loops at the top of the frame. Instead of forming the round loop though, bend the wires around the round-nose pliers so that they point straight upwards creating a U-bend.

5 Form a small round loop under the U-bend on either side (left earring in picture). Close the larger loops, as they will have opened slightly during the shaping (right earring in picture).

Tip: The small loops should sit away from the frame. This is important to allow the bead dangles to hang freely.

6 Begin coiling

Cut a piece of 28-gauge wire 30in (76cm) long. Attach it to the left of the frame by coiling three times, leaving a 1in (2.5cm) tail. Ensure the coils and chains are central and continue coiling approximately 45 times, until you reach the half loop.

Note: The chain will still be able to move around the frame; this will be fixed in place once the right hand side of the frame has been coiled. The weight of the bead dangles will ensure that it hangs nicely, once they are attached.

7 Secure the frame together

Follow the instructions for the *Mermaid's purse* earrings steps 9-17, binding the frame closed, forming the wrapped connector and attaching the briolettes on both frames.

8 Continue coiling

Coil the rest of the frame until you have 45 coils in total (the same as the left side) and ensuring that the central coils and chain are locked into place. Trim the length of wire and the 1in (2.5cm) tail and tuck the ends in on the inside of the frame.

9 Final step

Secure all the dangles in place. I have chosen to put one on each top loop, one at either end of the chain and three in the centre of the chain. Now attach the coiled earwires.

Variations

Experiment with the position of the dangles to achieve different looks. You could even attach a $^3/_{16}$in (4mm) bead to the frame above the briolette. Faceted briolettes add even more sparkle. Using handmade figure-of-eight chains gives a very structured look to the design.

CRESCENT
FIVE-BEAD RING

Unlike the Vortex wrapped ring, you form and shape this ring shank before embellishing it. This gives you a strong, rigid frame to work on. It calls for accurate shaping to ensure all the beads fit. You will find this is a very comfortable design to wear, since the ring only widens at the front.

Materials
- 8½in (22cm) 18-gauge soft round wire
- 40in (1.02m) 28-gauge soft or half-hard round wire
- Two ⅛in (3mm) round beads
- Two ³⁄₁₆in (4mm) round beads
- One ⁵⁄₁₆in (6mm) round bead

Tools
- Chain-nose pliers
- Flat-nose pliers
- Wire cutters
- Ring mandrel
- Sanding pads
- Pair of compasses
- Protractor
- Fine marker pen
- Pencil and paper
- Tape measure/ruler

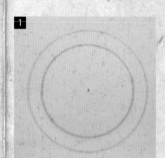

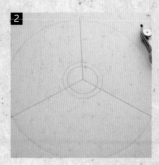

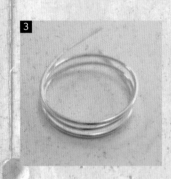

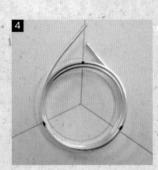

1 Make a template

In order to shape the ring accurately, the first thing to do is make a template to work against. Set your pair of compasses to ³/₈in (9.5mm) and draw a circle on your piece of paper. Reset the compasses to ¹/₂in (1cm) and draw a second circle using the same centre point. These are the circles you will use to line the ring up against.

2

Now draw a third larger circle again using the same centre point, setting your compasses against the protractor's centre and its outer edge. Use the protractor to mark out three points that are 120° apart on the outer circle. Now draw three lines from these points to the centre of the circle. Your template is now ready to use.
Tip: You can add as many different sized circles as you like to suit different sized rings.

3 Prepare the shank wire

Cut a piece of 18-gauge wire 8¹/₂in (22cm) long and straighten. Wrap the centre of the wire around the ring mandrel on UK size W (US size 11¹/₄) two-and-a-half times, so that you have three wraps on one half and two on the other half; both straight ends should be kept equal.
Tip: Due to the side coils and beads, the finished ring will be five sizes smaller than the starting size (using the suggested beads). Make sure you take this into account when planning your ring. This ring has a finished UK size of R (US size 8³/₄).

4

Line the ring up on your template. Use the marker pen to mark the three lines, dividing the ring into thirds. The bottom two marks are where you will form the side coils and the top mark is for the centre ⁵/₁₆in (6mm) bead. The bottom third will have three wires and the top two thirds will have two structure wires.

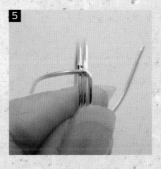

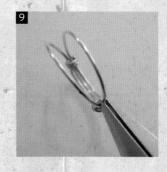

5 Secure the shank
Grasp one of the straight wires with your flat-nose pliers, level with your pen mark. Bend by 90° so that it crosses over the top of the two ring wires.

6 Hold the three wires from the bottom of the shank in place with the chain-nose pliers and wrap three times. Trim the wire so that the end is tapered and sand smooth with your sanding pads.

7 Repeat on the other side. Tip: Use the flat-nose pliers to help you wrap the wire. Do not pull too tightly though, as the three wires need to sit neatly next to each other.

8 Finish shaping
Measure 1/2in (1cm) either side of the top pen mark and make another pen mark. The top mark is where the 5/16in (6mm) bead will be attached since this is the central point. The other two marks outline where the beads start and finish, ensuring they are central.

9 Bend the two top wires of the ring outwards fractionally (by approximately 10° each) using the flat-nose pliers.

10 Place the 5/16in (6mm) bead so that it sits in place inside the wires at the top, to ensure you have opened the wires enough.

11 Begin coiling
Cut a piece of 28-gauge wire 40in (1.02m) long. Measure 18in (46cm) along this wire and attach this point to one side of the ring (on the wire without the pen marks) just after the bends by coiling three times. Continue coiling until you reach the bends on the other side.

12 Continue coiling
Transfer the 28-gauge wire to the uncoiled frame wire by taking it over the current wire and under the new one and coiling. Continue until you reach the first pen mark.

13 Attach the first bead
Make sure your coiling is just past the pen mark (covering it up). Thread a 1/8in (3mm) bead onto the wire, then take the wire round the opposite side of the frame and back through the bead.

14 Ensure the bead is straight and sitting between the two ring wires. Pull the 28-gauge wire tightly until you feel it click into place between the existing coils.

15 Attach all the beads
Continue coiling and attaching beads until all five are secured in place. Coil 12 times between the 1/8in (3mm) and 3/16in (4mm) beads and 16 times between the 3/16in (4mm) and 5/16in (6mm) beads. Make sure your 5/16in (6mm) bead is in line with the central mark.

16 Final step
Continue coiling until you are level with the start of the coiling on the other side. Trim the wire and the 1in (2.5cm) tail and tuck the ends in.

Variation

This copper and turquoise ring is made with the same wire measurements but I have used two $^3/_{16}$in (4mm), two $^1/_4$in (5mm) and one $^5/_{16}$in (6mm) beads. Notice how the beads sit more proudly from the frame. The ring was formed on UK size V (US size 10$^3/_4$) and has a finished UK size of P (US size 8).

The wire measurements given are suitable for rings down to finished UK size G (US size 3$^3/_4$). Any smaller than this and you will need to use smaller beads or fewer beads as the space on the ring will be reduced.

DAISY
POST EARRINGS

If dangly, flamboyant earrings are not for you,
this pair of understated post earrings with a colourful
bead are the perfect choice.

This project teaches you how to form a wire cup frame
for the bead to sit inside. The structure is secured together
with 28-gauge wire, which also holds the bead in place and
adds an attractive detail.

Materials
- 9in (23cm) 20-gauge soft or half-hard round wire
- 24in (61cm) 28-gauge soft or half-hard round wire
- Two ³/₁₆in (4mm) or ¼in (5mm) round beads
- Two butterfly earring backs

Tools
- Chain-nose pliers
- Round-nose pliers
- Flat-nose pliers
- Nylon-jaw pliers
- Wire cutters
- File/sanding pads
- Marker pen
- Tape measure/ruler

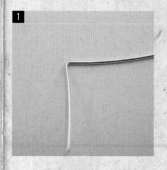

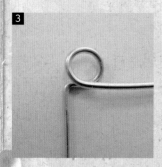

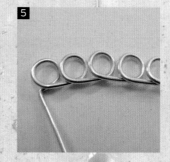

1 **Prepare the frame wires**
Cut a piece of 20-gauge
wire 4½in (12cm) long and
straighten. Measure ¾in
(2cm) from one end and make
a 90° bend using the flat-nose
pliers. This will be the post for
your earring.

2 Grasp the long length of
wire, just after the bend, with
your round-nose pliers. Wrap
the wire around the jaw to
form a complete circle.

3 The circle should measure
⅛in (3mm) across. I use the
centre point of the jaws on my
pliers to achieve this size.
Tip: Once you have found
the correct position on your
pliers, mark the jaw with the
marker pen so your loops will
be consistent in size.

4 **Form all the loops**
Grasp the long length of wire
with the round-nose pliers,
just after the first circle and
form another circle.

5 Repeat until you
have formed five circles
in total. Flatten them with
the nylon-jaw pliers.

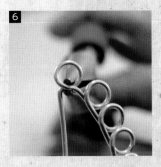

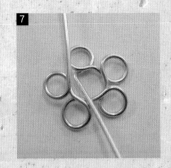

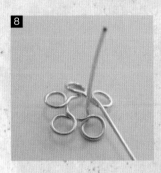

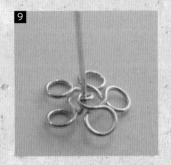

6 Form a circle of circles
Using the chain-nose pliers, grasp the wire at the point it crosses itself to secure the shape of the circle. Then carefully bend each loop away from the next one and work your way round so that the loops form a circle.

7 Ensure that the post lies on top of the circle.

8 Position the post
Using the flat-nose pliers, bend the post upwards so that it creates a 90° angle to the circle of loops (pointing straight upwards).

9 Coil the straight length of wire around the post once to close the circle and secure it in place. Trim and tuck the end. Take care that there are no sharp edges as this will sit against the ear!

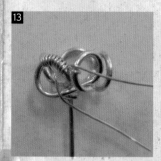

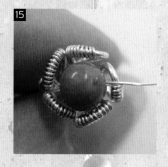

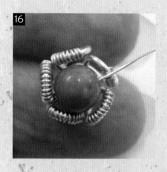

10 Shape the cup

Bend each loop upwards slightly using the flat-nose pliers, ensuring each loop overlaps the next one slightly, forming a cup shape.

Tip: Grasp the post with the nylon-jaw pliers to keep it straight and central whilst bending the loops.

11 Squeeze the loops into position with the nylon-jaw pliers, so that the cup is only just bigger than your bead.

12 Attach a new wire

Cut a piece of 28-gauge wire 12in (30cm) long. Attach it to the top of one loop, by coiling three times, leaving a 1in (2.5cm) tail to hold onto. Continue coiling until you reach the next loop.

13 Secure the loops together

Take the 28-gauge wire over the second loop and coil once, pulling tightly so that the two loops sit against each other, locking them together.

14 Continue coiling, working your way round each loop (coil 12 times per loop) until you are half way around the last loop.

15 Attach the bead

Thread the bead onto the 28-gauge wire. Then thread the wire through the opposite loop and back again through the bead.

16 Pull tightly to lock the wire into place.

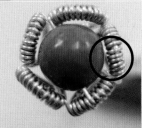

17 Continue coiling
Coil the frame as before until you reach where you started. Trim the wire and 1in (2.5cm) tail so that the ends meet and tuck them in.

18 Adjust post
Trim the post to $\frac{1}{2}$in (1cm) and file or sand the end so that it is smooth. Holding the post in the nylon-jaw pliers, check and adjust if necessary the position of the wire bead cup.

19 Final step
Slide the butterfly back onto the post, then make the second earring.

FERN FROND
BRIOLETTE NECKLACE

A beautiful fern in my garden unfurling its leaves one spring inspired the frame for this design. Several decoratively shaped wires are secured to a central structure wire with beads attached using a 'bird's nest setting' (see page 100) so that they are unable to move, creating a delicate, flowing necklace.

This project develops the skills and techniques you learnt in the *Butterfly wing* earrings project (see page 57).

Materials
- 6in (15cm) 18-gauge half-hard round wire
- 25in (63.5cm) 20-gauge soft or half-hard round wire (only 15in/38cm is required if you are using figure-of-eight chain)
- 60in (1.52m) 28-gauge soft or half-hard round wire
- Six ⅛in (3mm) beads
- Four ³⁄₁₆in (4mm) beads
- Three ⁵⁄₁₆mm (6mm) beads
- Three wrapped briolettes
- 15–45in (38–114cm) bought or handmade chain (depending on whether you use a single or triple strand)
- One clasp of your choice

Tools
- Chain-nose pliers
- Round-nose pliers
- Flat-nose pliers
- Nylon-jaw pliers
- Wire cutters
- Sanding pads (optional)
- Tape measure/ruler

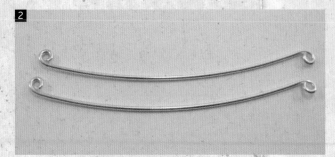

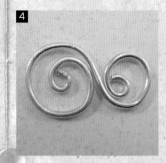

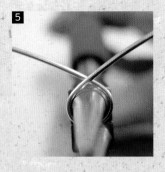

1 Preparation

Wrap the three briolette, following the *Wrapped briolette* instructions (see page 30). Ensure the loops face front to back, rather than side to side.

Cut four pieces of 20-gauge wire in preparation for the decorative detail to the following lengths:

- Two 2¹/₂in (6cm)
- One 4in (10cm)
- One 6in (15cm).

2 Begin to shape the decorative wires

Take the two pieces of 2¹/₂in (6cm) wire and form round loops at each end, facing in opposite directions.

3 Grasp one of the loops with the chain-nose pliers and carefully form an open spiral, using the jaw of the pliers to space the wire. Turn both your hands and the pliers at the same time, so that the shape is smooth and even. Rotate for one-and-a-half turns.

4 Form a smaller open spiral in the other end, in the opposite direction to the first, for one turn, forming an 'S' shape. Repeat in the other wire. Ensure both 'S' shapes are identical. Set aside.
Tip: These spirals can be tricky to shape when you are first learning, causing you to grip too tightly with the pliers and marking the wire. If this does happen, you can simply sand out any marks with the three grits of sanding pads before moving on to the next step.

5 Form the bottom loops

Using the thickest part of the round-nose pliers, form a loop in the centre of the 4in (10cm) piece of wire, so that the straight wires form a 'V' at the top that is a 90° angle approximately.

6 Form a smaller loop on either side, using the centre point of the jaws of the round-nose pliers, by grasping the straight wire just after the first loop and taking the wire over the top of itself.

7 Form two more loops either side, working your way down the jaws of the pliers, so that the loops gradually decrease in size. Do not flatten yet, as the briolette still needs to be attached. Set aside.

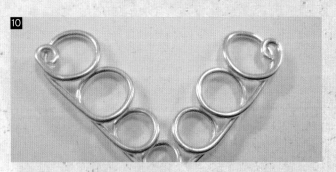

8 Shape the top loops

The loops on the top of the frame are formed in much the same way as the bottom ones, except that the loops point upwards and increase in size. Grasp the middle of the 6in (15cm) piece of wire with the centre of the jaw of the round-nose pliers. Wrap the wire one-and-a-half times around the jaw of the pliers, so that you have a double wire at the bottom of the loop.

9 Form three more loops either side, increasing gradually in size, ensuring you wrap the wire in the same direction each time, so that the loops form a straight line along the bottom.

10 Trim the straight wires to ¼in (5mm) from the last loop and then form a small round loop at each end. Flatten with your nylon-jaw pliers. Ensure the bottom edges remain straight and adjust with the chain-nose pliers if necessary. The straight edges should form a right angle. Set aside.

11 Attach a briolette

Carefully open the small loop on the bottom loops and thread one of the briolettes, working it round the loops until it is hanging from the central loop.

12 Close the small loop and flatten with the nylon-jaw pliers (taking care to avoid the briolette).

 13

 14

 15

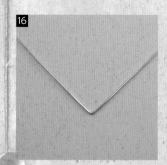 16

 17

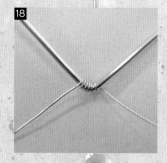 18

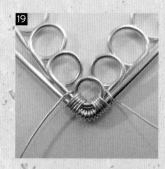 19

13 Secure the other briolettes

The two remaining briolettes are attached to the small spiral of the 'S' spirals. Carefully open the loop and thread the briolette on. Close the loop.

14 Cut a piece of 28-gauge wire 5in (13cm) long. Attach it to the 'S' spiral by coiling three times, leaving a 1in (2.5cm) tail.

15 Bind the larger spiral closed five times and the smaller spiral three times (see *Butterfly wing* earrings, page 57). Coil each three times to secure, trim and tuck the end in. Repeat on the second spiral.

16 Prepare the main frame wire

Cut a piece of 18-gauge wire 6in (15cm) long and straighten. Make a 90° bend in the centre (3in/7.5cm in from the end) using the flat-nose pliers, creating a large 'V' shape.

17 Lay all the components together as shown, checking that they fit and the angles are correct. Adjust if necessary.

18 Begin to attach the components

Cut a piece of 28-gauge wire 30in (76cm) long. Attach the centre (15in/38cm from the end) to the point of the main structure wire by coiling five times. Ensure the coiling is in the centre.

19 Hold the top loops in place and bind the central loop to the main structure wire five times on each side. The double thickness of the central loop should hold the structure wire in place beneath it.

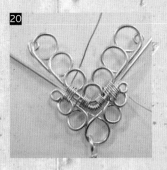

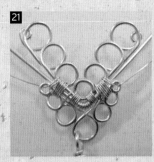

20 Attach the bottom loops
Hold the bottom loops against the main frame (taking care to hold the briolette out of the way, so that you don't get in a tangle). Bind the second loop either side of the bottom loops to the main structure wire and third loop of the top loops five times. Ensure that the wires sit neatly next to each other and the binding is neat and tight.

21 Bind the smallest loops on the bottom loop to the main frame and top loop twice.

22 Attach the 'S' spirals
Bind the small spiral of the 'S' spiral to the small bottom loop twice. This is important as it will stop the 'S' spiral from moving once it is attached to the main frame.

23 Bind the small spiral to the main frame three times. Continue binding until all loops and spirals are secured in place. Coil the main frame three times to secure. Repeat on the other side.
Tip: Although most of the binding will be hidden with beads, it is still important to keep it neat and tidy so that it is not only stronger but also so that the back of the piece is attractive and well finished too.

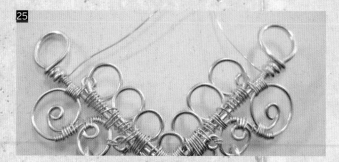

24 Finish the frame wires
Form a large loop in the main frame wire, on both sides, just after the large spiral.

25 Hold the loop in the chain-nose pliers and wrap the loop closed three times, using the flat-nose pliers to help you wrap the wire. Repeat on the other side. The frame should now be rigid.

26 Attach a bead
Now the frame is secured together you are ready to begin attaching beads. Cut a piece of 28-gauge wire 20in (50cm) long. Attach it to the left of the top central loop by binding the centre of the 28-gauge wire three times. (See circled area.)

27 Thread your central bead onto the wire and thread the wire through the central loop, pulling tightly, so that the bead is in the centre.

28 Wrap the bead
Pinch the wire running through the bead against the sides of the bead with your thumb and forefinger, so that the wrapping is able to sit tightly against the bottom of the bead. Wrap four times around the bottom of the bead, pulling tightly, so that the wire is not able to pass over the top of the bead, creating a 'bird's nest' setting. The bead should be rigid now.

29 Continue adding more beads
Secure the next three beads in place in the same way:
1   Thread the wire through a top loop
2   Thread a bead
3   Pass the wire through a bottom loop
4   Wrap the bead four times
5   Pass the wire back through a bottom loop, then through a top loop, ready for the next bead.

30 Once you have four beads in total, coil the nearest loop three times and trim (as you will have run out of wire).

31 Secure all the other beads
To attach the final bead on the right side, bring the remaining 28-gauge wire from securing the frame together through the small loop at the top. Secure the bead in place. Coil the nearest loop three times, trim and tuck in.

32 Secure the four beads on the left in place. The piece should be rigid and solid now.

33 Final step
Attach your chain and clasp using wrapped links with co-ordinating beads. If you are using figure-of-eight chain, you can attach this directly to the centrepiece. I have chosen to use three strands of chain for this piece. You could use a single strand of chain or create a loop of chain threaded through the loops of the centrepiece and attach this to the necklace chain with wrapped connectors.
Note: Using 7¹/₂in (19cm) of chain will give you an 18–20in (46–50cm) necklace, depending on how many connectors you use (if using figure-of-eight chain it will be an 18in/46cm necklace).

Variations
You can add as many briolettes as you like and experiment with the size of the beads; using all one size gives a very chic look to the design. You can also make matching earrings, following the instructions for the 'S' spirals and attaching an earwire to the large spiral. To make the highly wrapped briolettes shown on these variations, see *The vine pendant* (page 164).

BOUDICA
SPIRAL BRACELET

Inspired by the warrior queen herself, this bracelet has a strong Celtic influence and is made from three identical discs.

This project teaches you how to make open 'S' spiral shapes and attach them to the double spiral frame (which is constructed from a single wire) – all of which are shaped by hand.

The structure wire is shaped as you work rather than forming it in advance for two reasons. It makes it easier to attach the spirals and coil the frame but also you can achieve a much more accurate shape.

Materials
- 45¼in (1.15m) of 16-gauge soft or half-hard round wire
- 12in (30cm) of 18-gauge soft or half-hard round wire
- 27¾in (70.5cm) 20-gauge soft round wire
- 435in (11.1m) 28-gauge soft or half-hard round wire

Tools
- Chain-nose pliers
- Round-nose pliers
- Flat-nose pliers
- Nylon-jaw pliers
- Wire cutters
- Pair of compasses
- Hammer
- Anvil
- Bracelet mandrel (or homemade alternative – see 'Tools and Materials' section, page 12)
- Tape measure

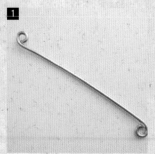

 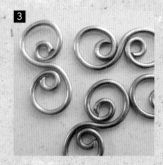

1 Preparation

The first thing you need to do is make all of the 'S' spirals. For each disc there are four large 'S' spirals, one small and one tapered figure-of-eight link. For the large spirals, cut a piece of 20-gauge wire 1³⁄₄in (4.5cm) long. Make a round loop at each end (see *Simple earwires*, page 20), so that the loops are in opposite directions.

Tip: I tend to make everything needed for the three discs at the same time; this way you can ensure they are all exactly the same size. If you choose to work this way you will need:

- 12 large 'S' spirals
- Three small 'S' spirals
- Three tapered figure-of-eight links.

2 Grasp one loop with the chain-nose pliers, just past the point where the loop closes. Using the jaw of the pliers to space the spiral, take the wire round for one complete circle, so that the top of the loop is open and the bottom sits against the loop as shown. Repeat on the other side, making sure you are working in the opposite direction to the first.

3 Ensure the loops are in a straight line to each other. Tip: The second spiral will be more difficult to form than the first one as the wire becomes work hardened. To make it easier, hold the first spiral between the flat-nose pliers while you form the second one with the chain-nose pliers. You may need to re-adjust the first spiral if it becomes misshapen while forming the second.

4 Your finished spirals should be ¹⁄₂in (1cm) long. Make four in total for one disc or 12 for three discs. Tip: To ensure they are all equal and evenly sized, stack them all up (making sure they are all facing the same direction) so you can clearly see any adjustments that are required.

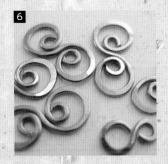

5 Form the spirals for the tapered end

As the finished disc tapers at the edge, the spirals need to progressively decrease in size. The smaller spiral is made in exactly the same way as the larger ones, but uses a shorter piece of wire, so that the finished spiral is fractionally smaller.

Cut a piece of 20-gauge wire 1½in (4cm) long and form an 'S' spiral as in steps 1–4. This smaller spiral should measure ⅓in (8.5mm) when finished. Also form the tapered figure of eight (see *Figure-of-eight links and chain*, page 24) using ¾in (2cm) 20-gauge wire – the larger loop should use ½in (1cm) wire and the smaller ¼in (5mm).

Tip: If you struggle to keep the shapes flat while you are forming them, don't worry – just give them a squeeze between the nylon-jaw pliers when you are done.

6 Hammer

Carefully flatten each spiral by gently hammering each one (see *Hook and 'S' clasp*, page 34). Flatten both ends of each spiral and very slightly in the centre. Set aside.

Note: You may need to re-adjust the spirals once you have done this as the hammering action tends to force the spirals open.

7 Prepare the frame

Cut a piece of 16-gauge wire 14in (35.5cm) long. Straighten the wire (see *Simple earwires* page 20). Measure half way along the wire (7in/18cm) and grasp with the thickest point on the jaws of your round-nose pliers. Take the right hand wire round the bottom jaw and the left hand wire over the top jaw forming a giant 'S'.

8 Begin to form the double spiral

Holding the frame wire in the jaws of the round-nose pliers, begin to form the spiral shape, by holding one end of the wire and curling it loosely round the central shape for a quarter turn. Repeat on the other end, this time making the spiral a little tighter.

9 Ensure the two wire ends are at opposite sides of the shape at all times, this will make it easier to achieve an even shape.

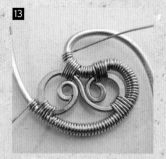

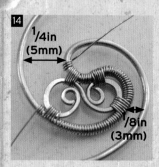

1/4in
(5mm)

1/8in
(3mm)

10 Prepare to attach the first spiral

Gently loosen off the top straight wire, thus enlarging the bottom loop slightly. Check that one of the 'S' spirals fits neatly inside (remember to allow room for the coiled 28-gauge wire on either side). Adjust if necessary, by loosening the loop more.

11 Attach a thin wire

We have now completed all the preparation work and are ready to begin assembly. Cut a piece of 28-gauge wire 45in (1.14m) long. Attach it to the large loop on the frame by coiling the centre of the thin wire (so you have 22½in/57cm each side) 20 times, ensuring your coiling is tight and neat (see *Butterfly wing* earrings, page 57).

12 Attach the first spiral

Bind each side of the first spiral to the frame six times, holding the spiral in place between your thumb and forefinger. Ensure your binding is neat and do not pull too tightly as the spiral must sit inside the frame. *Note: The binding will pull the spiral out of line with the frame.*

13 Secure the spiral in place

Coil the top structure wire five times and the bottom one 25 times (this allows for the curvature of the wires). The thin wire should now be in line with the second spiral top and bottom. Bind both sides of the spiral six times. It is now firmly secured in place.

14 Shape the frame

After attaching each spiral, you need to shape the frame a little more in preparation for attaching the next spiral. Holding the end of the frame wire (this will give you a smoother shape) bend each end round the central detail for a quarter turn. The open spiral should have a ⅛in (3mm) gap and the decorated spiral should have a ¼in (5mm) gap. Coil the top wire three times and the bottom one 20 times.

15 Attach the second spiral

Lay the second spiral in the frame to check it fits. Adjust the frame if necessary. Attach in the same way as the first, by binding six times at each of the four points it touches the frame.

16 Attach the next two spirals

Continue working in this way until you have secured all four of the larger spirals.
Tip: Coil 15–20 times on the outer frame wire and three to five times on the inner one between each spiral, making sure the coiling is level both sides as you work your way round the frame.

17

Cut a new piece of 28-gauge wire 25in (63.5cm) long. Lock the new wire into the coils of the old wire (for about three coils), leaving a 1in (2.5cm) tail and ensuring the new wire follows the same direction as the old. This will stop the wire slipping and help to hide the join.
Note: You will need to attach new coiling wires from time to time. To do this trim the old wire so that it is on the inside of the frame. Then tuck the end in with the chain-nose pliers.

18

After attaching each spiral, shape the frame wire another quarter turn. In order to check your disc is circular, draw a template using a pair of compasses set to ³⁄₄in (2cm), which will give you a circle 1½in (4cm) across.

19

Every time you shape the frame, offer it up to the template to check it is circular. It will also make shaping the taper at the end much easier.

20 Attach the tapering spiral

Shape the frame wire another quarter turn. Check it against your template – the circle should be almost complete. Secure the small 'S' spiral and tapered figure-of-eight in place, this time binding three times instead of six on the inside of the 'S' spiral and three times each side for the figure-of-eight, to allow for the smaller shapes.

21 Shape the taper

Trim any 1in (2.5cm) tails of 28-gauge wire and carefully tuck the ends in so that they are on the inside of the frame and thus hidden. Shape the frame against your template, creating the tapered edge to the spiral. Take care not to pull the wire too tightly as you will run the risk of pushing the 'S' spirals out of place inside the frame. If this does happen, loosen the frame slightly and use your nylon-jaw pliers to push them back into place.

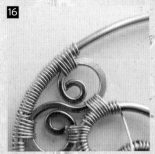
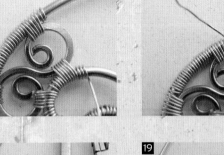

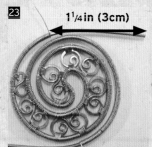

1¼in (3cm)

22 Coil

Continue coiling both sides of the disc until you are in line with the start of the spiral. *Note: You will have to coil one side more than the other.*

23 Form the loops

Now that the disc shape is complete you need to form the loops on either side. Trim the straight structure wires to 1¼in (3cm) from the end of the coiling.

24 Form a large loop using the thickest point on your round-nose pliers so that the loop begins exactly where the coiling stops. *Note: You may need to gently pull the structure wires away from the disc to allow you room to fit the pliers in.*

25 Form a tiny round loop (using the very tip of your round-nose pliers) inside the larger loop.

26 Flatten the loops into place with your nylon-jaw pliers. Readjust the structure wires again, so that the loops sit neatly against the disc.

27 Bind the loops

Bind both loops to the main disc frame four times and then coil the outer loop four times, to secure the thin wire in place. Trim and tuck the ends in. Notice how sturdy this makes the disc.

28 Hammer the outer edge of both large loops.

29 Shape the disc

Carefully shape the disc around your bracelet mandrel (or your homemade cylindrical object – see 'Tools and Materials' page 12) by pressing it into place with your fingers, while holding it in place with your other hand, to create a slight curve.

30 Make two more discs, taking care that when you come to shaping them, they are facing the same direction as the first. To ensure all three discs are identical, use the first one you made as your template for the other two – this way you can ensure all your spirals are in the same position and that the overall shape and size is exactly the same.

31 Make the connectors and clasp

Make 12 figure-of-eight connectors using pieces of 18-gauge wire 1in (2.5cm) long and a tapered figure-of-eight connector using a piece of 16-gauge wire 1¼in (3cm) long (see *Figure-of-eight chain*, page 24). Make a hook clasp using a piece of 16-gauge wire 2in (5cm) long (see *Hook and 'S' clasp*, page 34). Hammer all the pieces to flatten them slightly. This not only hardens the wire and adds interest to the texture of the wire but also allows the links to sit neatly against each other where you are using multiple links for one connection.

32 Final step

Connect all of the pieces together, with three figure-of-eight links for each connection, ensuring they are all facing the same direction. Attach the clasp and connector to the end of the bracelet.

Variations

The dimensions in this project will give you a 7½in (19cm) bracelet. If you would like a larger one, just add extra connectors between the discs and clasp.

For an alternative design, make one disc and attach three lengths of figure of eight chain to either side, each measuring 1⅔in (4.2cm) with a large figure-of-eight connector on each end.

AMMONITE
SPIRAL PENDANT

This is a great design for dressing up a relatively plain bead into something stunning.

Two contrasting weaves are used to make a frame for an oval bead, with the woven spiral being the main focus of the pendant. The detail on the front of the frame also holds your bead in position, stopping it from turning in its setting.

This project develops the skills you learnt in the *Orbital* pendant (see page 65), as you learn to weave on a curve and with a second, simple, contrasting weave pattern.

Materials
- 10in (25cm) 18-gauge soft round wire
- 75in (1.9m) 28-gauge soft or half-hard round wire
- One flat oval bead, approximately ¾in (2cm) tall x ⅝in (1.5cm) wide and ¼in (5mm) deep

Tools
- Chain-nose pliers
- Round-nose pliers
- Flat-nose pliers
- Wire cutters
- Nylon-jaw pliers
- Pin/needle
- ⅛in (3mm) diameter mandrel (kebab stick, knitting needle, wooden dowel, etc) (optional)

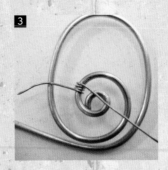

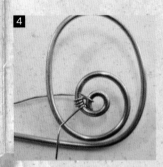

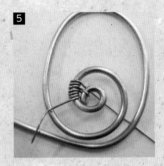

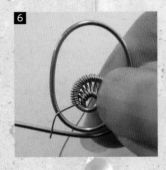

1 Prepare the first frame wire

The frame around the bead is made from two structure wires. One forming the spiral design on the front and the second skims the outer edge of the bead and forms the bail. To form the spiral frame, cut a 4in (10cm) piece of 18-gauge wire and straighten. Form a medium round loop at one end. Using the chain-nose pliers, form an open spiral for one full rotation around the loop.

2

Carefully shape the straight wire around the bead, so that it completes the oval shape of the frame. Do not finish the end of the wire yet; instead leave the frame open, making it easier to weave the spiral.

Tip: Ensure that the frame is slightly smaller than the bead and sits on top of it.

3 Weave the spiral

Cut a piece of 28-gauge wire 15in (38cm) long. Attach it to your spiral, just above where the loop closes, by coiling three times, leaving a 1in (2.5cm) tail.

4

The weave needs to take into account the curve of the spiral. So take the 28-gauge wire over the spiral wire and under the loop wire, through the loop and back under the spiral wire. Notice that the loop is not coiled.

5

Now coil the spiral wire three times, pulling tightly to lock the wire in place.

6 Continue weaving

Keep weaving in this way:
- Coil outer spiral three times
- Pass over the outer wire and under the loop
- Pass through the loop and back under the outer spiral wire.

Continue all the way around the loop.

Ensure you keep the weave tight by sliding it around the frame with your thumbnail.

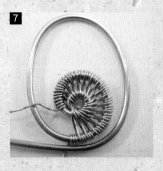

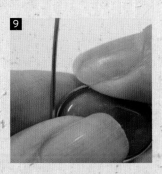

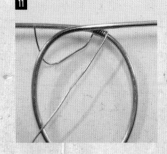

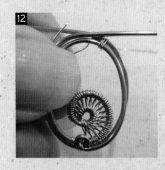

7 Notice how the extra coiling keeps the weave straight and prevents it from being on a slant.

8 Close the frame

Now the weaving is complete on the spiral, the frame needs to be closed to secure its shape. Trim the straight wire to 1/4in (5mm) from the edge of the weaving, checking the frame is still the correct size and has not become misshapen during the weaving. Form a round loop that overlaps the frame. Bind the loop to the frame three times to secure in place. Coil the frame three times to secure the wire, trim the wire and its 1in (2.5cm) tail and tuck the ends in.

9 Prepare the main frame Cut 6in (15cm) of 18-gauge wire and straighten. Position the centre of the wire against the bottom of the bead and carefully shape around the bead using your fingers.

10 The straight wires should cross at the top of the frame, which should fit perfectly around the edge of the bead. Both straight wires should be at least 1 1/2in (4cm) long (to form the bail with later).
Note: The spiral frame should be fractionally smaller than the main frame.

11 Secure the two frames together

Cut a piece of 28-gauge wire 35in (89cm) long and attach it to the top right of the main frame by coiling six times, leaving a 1in (2.5cm) tail.

12 Hold the two frames in position between the thumb and forefinger of your less dominant hand, then bind the frames together three times. Don't pull too tightly as there needs to be enough room between the two frames for the 28-gauge wire to pass between them.
Tip: Although the binding is used to attach the two frame wires together, it is also part of the decorative finish, so it is very important that it is neat and straight. To achieve this, keep the 28-gauge wire at a 90° angle to the frames.

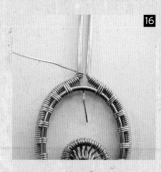

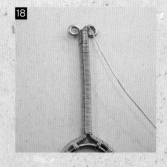

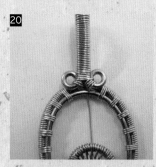

13 Continue round the frame

Work your way around the frame, coiling six times then binding three times. Push the binding and coiling tightly together to ensure the spacing is even. Notice how quickly the pattern forms.

14 Continue until the frame is complete.

Tip: When you get to the spiral, you may need to bend this upwards slightly, so that it is more central in the frame, allowing you enough room for the 28-gauge wire to pass between the woven spiral and frame to bind it.

15 Prepare the bail wires

Trim and tuck in the 28-gauge wire and its 1in (2.5cm) tail. Using the flat-nose pliers, bend the straight wires upwards 90° so that they sit parallel to each other, ensuring that the wires are straight.

16 Bind the bail

Cut a piece of 28-gauge wire 25in (63.5cm) long and attach it to one of the bail wires by coiling three times, leaving a 1in (2.5cm) tail.

17 Bind the two bail wires

together with the 28-gauge wire, ensuring the binding is neat and straight and that the bail wires remain parallel to each other. Continue until you have covered 1in (2.5cm) of the bail wires. Coil one of the bail wires three times to secure the binding, but do not trim the wire.

18 Shape the bail

Trim the straight wires to 1/4in (5mm) from the top of the binding. Bend outwards by 45° and form two small round loops. Trim the 1in (2.5cm) tail and tuck the end in.

19 Measure half way along

the bail and using either your 1/8in (3mm) mandrel or your round-nose pliers, bend the wires downwards, forming a hook. Grasp the end of the bail (including the two loops) with the flat-nose pliers and bend upwards by 45°. Pinch the bail closed so the loops sit flush against the frame.

20 Close the bail

Use the 28-gauge wire to secure the bail closed, by passing the wire through the gap between the spiral frame and the bail, then through a loop, pulling tightly to lock into position. Repeat this four times in total (twice through each loop).

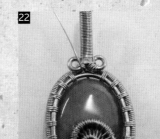

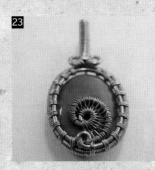

Variations
- Add small metal beads of graduating sizes after the spiral
- Weave the bail instead of binding
- Add a 1/8in (3mm) metal bead to the bail and secure in position with a bird's nest setting
- Experiment with different shaped beads.

21 Secure the bead
First thread the bead onto the wire. Pass the 28-gauge wire between the two frame wires at the bottom and back through the bead.

22 Pull tightly to lock it into place.
Tip: You may find that you need to push a pin or needle between the two frame wires in order to create enough room for the 28-gauge wire to pass through.

23 Final step
Pass the 28-gauge wire through one of the loops (preferably the one that has not yet been coiled) and coil three times to secure, trim and tuck the end in.

ADVANCED PROJECTS

The projects in this section are designed to really challenge you. It is very important that you have mastered all of the techniques covered in previous sections of the book before attempting these projects.

Below is a list of the projects in this section and the skills and techniques they cover:

Sea urchin
- Forming a complicated frame
- Setting an undrilled stone (cabochon)
- Weaving and shaping a ring shank

Lace
- Forming and shaping a thick wire frame cuff
- Creating detail with wire shapes
- Securing together

Poseidon
- Creating a free form setting for an undrilled flat stone
- Using wire detail to secure the stone in place
- Forming a woven bail that is independent from the pendant

Eclipse
- Securing spirals together without a frame wire
- Creating a bezel wire
- Setting a cabochon

Gorgon
- Layering multiple structure wires and intertwining them
- Weaving on a curve

Orchid
- Creating a 3D design using multiple structure wires
- Attaching beads to weaving
- Shaping the weave

The vine – how to develop a design
The main project shows you how to make a pendant, then develop the design theory into the following:
- Earring
- Donut bail
- Cuff
- Necklace

SEA URCHIN
WOVEN RING

A prong setting is the classic way to set an undrilled
stone, but with this project we take a fresh approach
by making the prongs the main feature of the design.
Detail is added by weaving, while wrapped connectors lock
the prongs into position. This is a large, statement ring
that is bound to attract attention.

This technique can be used for setting stones in
all types of jewelry.

Materials
- 19in (48cm) 20-gauge
  soft round wire
- 148in (3.76m) 28-gauge
  soft or half-hard round
  wire
- One 1 x ¹¹/₁₆in (2.5 x 1.8cm)
  oval cabochon

Tools
- Chain-nose pliers
- Round-nose pliers
- Flat-nose pliers
- Nylon-jaw pliers
- Wire cutters
- Ring mandrel
- Pin/needle
- Tape measure

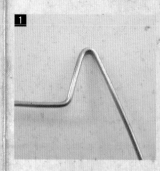

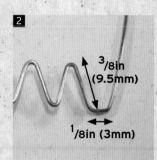

3/8in (9.5mm)

1/8in (3mm)

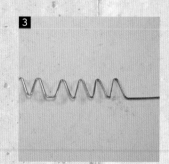

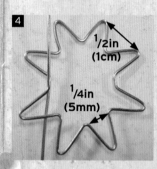

1/2in (1cm)

1/4in (5mm)

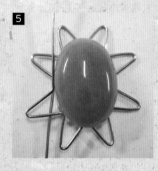

1 Shape the prongs

The ring is constructed using two structure wires, one for the prongs and one for the base wire. These are secured together using 28-gauge wire. The first thing to do is form the prongs. Cut a piece of 20-gauge wire 11in (28cm) long to make the prongs. Measure 3½in (9cm) from the end of the wire (this will be used later for the shank) and make a 70° bend using the flat-nose pliers. Measure ³⁄₈in (9.5mm) from this bend and now make a sharp 135° bend downwards, forming the first prong.

2 Complete the top edge

Form another three prongs in the same way, so that there are four in total, creating a zigzag pattern. This is the top half of the ring. You need to leave a gap in the prongs, for the shank to be attached to. Measure ³⁄₈in (9.5mm) from the last bend on the fourth prong and bend the wire upwards by 70°. Measure ¹⁄₈in (3mm) from this bend and bend upwards by 45°.

3 Complete the frame

Form another four prongs, taking care they are all identical in size. Once you have formed the last prong, bend the wire upwards by 70° so that it forms a straight line with the 3½in (9cm) wire at the start.

4

Now the prongs are formed, the frame needs to be shaped, to match the oval cabochon. Open the gap between each prong to ½in (1cm) at the top, ensuring each prong remains ¼in (5mm) wide at the bottom.

5

The cabochon should fit perfectly in the centre and overlap the bottom of each prong.

6 Form the main frame

Cut a piece of 20-gauge wire 8in (20cm) long. Measure 3½in (9cm) along the wire (this will be used for the shank) and line this point up with the side of the cabochon. Wrap the wire around the edge of the cabochon, so that you form a frame that is ¹⁄₁₆in (2mm) smaller than the stone.

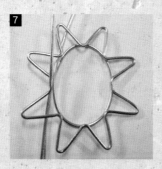

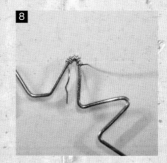

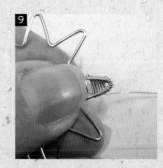

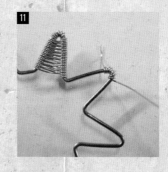

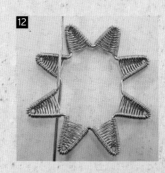

7 Line the two frames up together. The inside of the prong frame should be touching the main frame.

8 Weave the prongs

Each prong needs to be woven individually before the two frames are attached together. Each prong uses 8½in (22cm) of 28-gauge wire to weave it. I work with 25in (63.5cm) (enough for three prongs) at a time, to reduce wastage. Attach the 28-gauge wire to the tip of one of the prongs by coiling seven times. This is important as it will create the gap for the wrapped connectors to pass through.

9 Weave the prong in the same way as you did for the *Orbital* pendant (see page 65) – over, under, coil once – pulling tightly to lock into place. Tip: Weaving in closed spaces can be tricky. Think of the end of the wire as a needle and thread it through the space, taking care that the wire does not form a loop, as this will become a kink and ruin your weave. Use your thumbnail to guide the wire into place. If you struggle to tighten the weave, use a ratchet motion – pull the wire round, release upwards without releasing any pressure and then pull round again.

10 Continue until you reach the bottom of the prong, then coil one side three times to secure it.

11 Weave all the prongs

Trim the 28-gauge wire and 1in (2.5cm) tail and tuck the ends in on the inside of the frame. Re-attach the 28-gauge wire to the top of the next prong, by coiling seven times and weave.

12 Continue like this until all of the prongs are woven. Notice how strong the prongs have now become.
Tip: Ensure you have at least 8½in (22cm) of 28-gauge wire when starting a new prong; any less and you will need to cut a new length of wire – you don't want to run out mid weave!

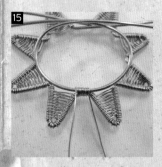

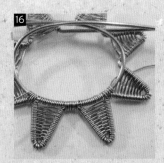

13 Open the tips of the prongs
To ensure there is room to construct the wrapped connectors later, push a pin or needle through the gap in the top of each prong, to open it up.

14 Secure the two frames together
Lay the frame wires together, so that the short wire from each frame points in opposite directions. Check that the frames are still the correct size and shape and that the prong frame has not become misshapen during the weaving.

15 Cut a 30in (76cm) length of 28-gauge wire and attach the centre of this to the ¼in (5mm) gap, binding the two frames together eight times.

16 Continue working around the frame, coiling the oval frame 12–15 times between each prong and binding each prong in place three times until all the prongs are secured apart from the final bend on the prongs either side of the cross-over wires.

17 Work on each side alternately, to ensure the frames are attached evenly.

18 Close the frame
Bend the two short wires outwards, away from the frame by 90° and trim down to 1in (2.5cm). Bend the two long wires upwards by 90°. Bind the two final edges of the prongs in place three times. Coil one of the thin wires around the nearest thick wire three times to secure and trim. Using the other thin wire, bind the two long wires together three times and coil one of the wires three times and trim. Check your frame is still straight and the prongs are symmetrical.

19 Weave the shank
Cut a piece of 28-gauge wire 30in (76cm) long. Attach it to the long wire that has not yet been coiled, by coiling three times, leaving a 1in (2.5cm) tail.

20 Weave for 1½in (4cm). Then coil one wire three times to secure. Do not trim.
Tip: Check the shank wires are straight and parallel before you start weaving.

21 Secure the stone
Hold the frame in your less dominant hand, so that the shank points downwards between your index and middle finger. Position the stone and hold it firmly in place with your thumb.

22 Carefully bend alternate prongs up around the stone. Work your way round gradually. Keep checking the stone is in the correct position, until all the prongs are pointing upwards. The stone should already be held firmly in place.

23 Finish shaping the prongs
The tip of each prong needs to be shaped around the stone, using the nylon-jaw pliers. Work on alternate prongs, so that you do not push the stone out of line.

24 Don't push the prongs tightly against the stone just yet, as you still need to form the wrapped connectors.
Tip: Take your time with this stage and keep checking the stone is lined up correctly and that the prongs have an equal gap between them.

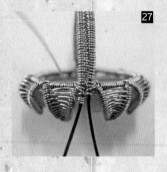

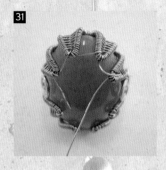

25 Form two spirals
In the two short wires, form the spirals, so that one sits above the other. Push them against the stone for now, as they will be repositioned once the shank is formed.

26 Form the shank
Position the stone and setting squarely on the ring mandrel and wrap the shank around UK size K (US size 5 ½).
Note: If you would like a larger or smaller ring, to calculate the length of shank you need, measure the circumference of the mandrel on your required size, in this case 2¼in (5.5cm), minus the width of the stone and its setting (³⁄₄in/2cm). This leaves 1½in (4cm) – the length of your shank.

27 Bind in place
Bind the shank in place to the ¼in (5mm) gap in the prongs, using the leftover wire from weaving. Make sure you pull the 28-gauge wire tightly, so that it holds the shank and locks into place between the existing bindings.

28 Once secured, trim the straight wires to 1in (2.5cm) and form two spirals.

29 Position the spirals
Check the shank is still the correct size on the mandrel and adjust by tightening or loosening the spirals if necessary. Bend the lowest spiral down, over the join of the shank on each side and push the other spiral between the prongs against the stone.

30 Connect the prongs
To secure the prongs in position (as they could get caught on things if left in their current position, causing them to open up), cut a 20in (50cm) length of 28-gauge wire. Attach it to the tip of a prong by coiling twice, leaving a 1in (2.5cm) tail.

31 Hold the tail in place, against the stone and thread the wire through the tip of the next prong, making sure you thread in the same direction as the first.

32 Work your way around the ring twice, pulling the wire tightly.
Tip: You may need to lift the prongs slightly to pass the wire through. Use a pin or needle to enlarge the hole if necessary.

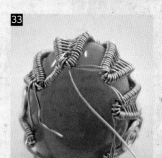

Variations

This variation has shorter prongs, making the wrapped connectors longer. I have given the connectors a slight curve to add shape to them. Also notice that the space between each prong is larger, showing off more of the stone.

The technique can be used to make pendants too. Below are two variations, one with tiny silver beads between each prong and one with wrapped connectors.

33 Wrap the connectors
To secure the connectors and make them more attractive, coil them together. Once you reach the next prong, thread the wire through the tip and coil the next one.

34 Work your way round the ring. Once you reach the end of the last connector, trim the wire and the 1in (2.5cm) tail and tuck the ends in.

35 Final step
Flatten each prong against the stone with the nylon-jaw pliers, pushing the wrapped connectors into position too.

LACE
FILIGREE-INSPIRED CUFF

I have always loved filigree jewelry and, with its flowing spirals contrasted with intricate detail, this cuff is heavily influenced by the style. I developed this cuff design from one of my early rings at the suggestion of my dear friend Jodi Bombardier. As she is the queen of cuffs, the ends of this one were inspired by Jodi's beautiful work.

The finished size is 7 1/4 in (18.5cm).

Materials
- 19in (48cm) 16-gauge soft or half-hard round wire
- 32in (81cm) 18-gauge soft or half-hard round wire
- 150in (3.8m) 24-gauge soft round wire
- 96in (2.44m) 28-gauge soft or half-hard round wire
- Two 1/8in (3mm) round metal beads
- Two 3/16in (4mm) round metal beads

Tools
- Chain-nose pliers
- Round-nose pliers
- Flat-nose pliers
- Nylon-jaw pliers
- Wire cutters
- Protractor
- Oval bracelet mandrel
- Rawhide mallet
- Pin/needle
- Tape measure

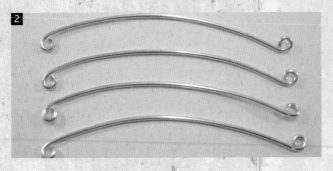

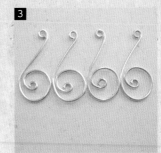

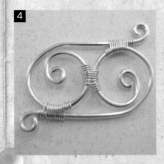

1 Begin to form the wire detail

Before you begin to construct the cuff, all the wire detail needs to be prepared. Follow the instructions for the *Butterfly wing* earrings (see page 57), using two pieces of 18-gauge wire 3in (7.5cm) long and one piece of 10in (25cm) 28-gauge wire, forming the detail for each end of the cuff. Set aside.

2 Form the yin and yang spirals

Cut four pieces of 18-gauge wire 3in (7.5cm) long. Form a round loop at each end, in opposite directions.

3 Then at one end of each piece of wire, form a large open spiral, so that each spiral measures 1in (2.5cm) long in total.

4 Secure two of the spirals together so that you have a straight edge top and bottom and the spirals meet in the middle. Using 13in (33cm) of 28-gauge wire, bind the straight edge of each piece to the spiral of the second piece nine times, coiling three times at the start and finish of the binding to secure. Then bind the spirals together in the middle six times.

5 Repeat with the other two spirals. These shapes will sit either side of the cuff, just after the double spirals. Set aside.

6 Form the central detail

Cut an 8in (20cm) length of 18-gauge wire and straighten. Measure 3in (7.5cm) from one end and make a sharp bend using the flat-nose pliers. Pinch the bend together with the pliers.

7 Open the bend up to form a 45° angle. Grasp the wire just after the bend with the round-nose pliers and bend the wire round the jaw. Repeat on the other side of the bend, forming a leaf shape that is 1/2in (1cm) long and 1/4in (5mm) wide.

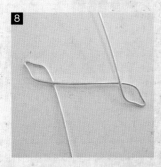

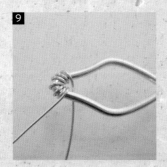

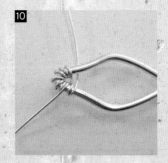

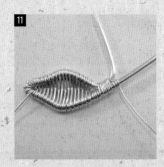

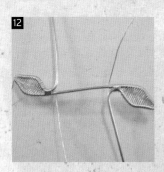

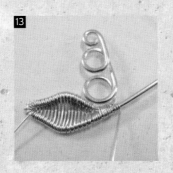

8 Repeat steps 6 and 7 at the other end of the wire in the opposite direction to the first leaf. The straight wire between the two leaves should be 1in (2.5cm) long.

9 Weave the leaves
Cut 25in (63.5cm) of 28-gauge wire. Attach it to the tip of one of the leaf shapes, by coiling it around six times, leaving a 1in (2.5cm) tail.

10 Weave in the same way as the *Orbital* pendant (see page 65) – over, under, coil once. Keep the weave neat and tight, until you reach the point where the wires cross. Coil three times to secure.

11 Bend the 3in (7.5cm) straight wire 160° back on itself, bind the two structure wires together seven times to close the leaf and coil the central structure wire three times to secure. Do not trim the wire.

12 Repeat on the second leaf.

13 Form loops
Starting in the centre of the jaws of your round-nose pliers, form three tapered loops (see Fern Frond briolette necklace step 6 and 7, page 96) in the 3in (7.5cm) straight wires either side, so that the total length is ½in (1cm).

14 Shape the central loops
The centre detail is constructed with two sets of tapered loops that are attached to the 1in (2.5cm) central wire between the leaves. Cut two 3in (7.5cm) pieces of 18-gauge wire and straighten. Grasp the centre of the wire with the round-nose pliers and form a loop that is ¼in (5mm) tall.

15 Form two more tapered loops either side of the central loop on both pieces of wire, ensuring that the two pieces match in size and shape. They should be ⅝in (1.5cm) wide and ½in (1cm) tall. Flatten with the nylon-jaw pliers.

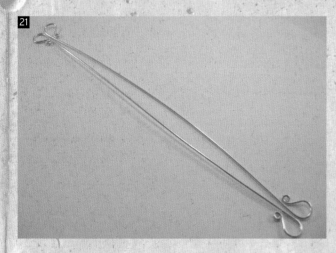

16 Attach to the leaves

Bend the wire just below the leaves by 45° in opposite directions, to form a 'Y' shape at each end of the central detail with the leaf and loops. This will give a central straight wire just over ½in (1cm) long to attach the central loops on to. Line the central loops up against the straight wire and coil the 28-gauge wire to the point where the small loops meet the straight wire on either side.

17

Bind the loops in place by taking the 28-gauge wire through the small loops either side three times. Coil the wire around the central straight wire twice each side to secure the binding. The central loops should still be able to move.

18 Add beads

Attach a ⅛in (3mm) bead either side with the 28-gauge wire, by threading the bead onto the wire and then coiling the central wire six times on each side. Ensure the bead is sitting on top of the central 18-gauge wire.

19

Thread the ³⁄₁₆in (4mm) beads onto the 28-gauge wire, thread the wire through the top loops and back through the bead. Repeat this on the other side. Coil the 28-gauge wires three times around the central straight wire to secure, trim and tuck in. Trim the 1in (2.5cm) tails on the leaves and tuck in. Set aside.

20 Prepare the main structure wires

Now all the detail is complete, you can begin to construct the cuff. Cut two pieces of 16-gauge wire 9½in (24cm) long and straighten. Form round loops at each end of the wire ⅛in (3mm) wide, facing in the same direction. Check both pieces are identical in length. Grasp the wire with the round-nose pliers, just after the loop (using the thickest part of the jaw), then bend the wire round in the opposite direction to the loop.

21

Repeat at each end of the wire.

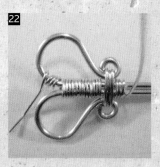

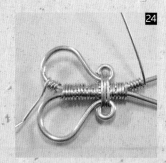

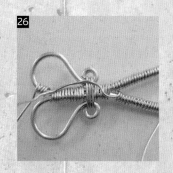

22 Secure the frame wires together

Cut two pieces of 24-gauge wire 25in (63.5cm) long. Attach one to one end of a frame wire, by coiling the hook three times, leaving a 1in (2.5cm) tail. Bind the two structure wires together 12 times. Bind through the two loops three times, and then bind the two straight wires three times. Repeat on the other end, securing the frame together.

Tip: Binding with 24-gauge wire is much harder than with 28-gauge wire as it is so much thicker. It is important to use soft wire. Also consider each placement of the wire, bending the wire around the frame, rather than just wrapping. Take your time and hold the binding in place with the thumb of your less dominant hand, while you position the new wrap with your dominant hand.

23 Shape the frame

Using the flat-nose pliers, bend each frame wire outwards by 20° (so an angle of 40° is formed between them), using the protractor to check your angles. This will create a nice curve in the frame, with the widest point being just over 1in (2.5cm).

24 Bind the two frame wires together another three times and coil the frame four times to secure.

25 Position the detail inside the frame, checking it all fits and adjusting if necessary. The frame should now be 7¼in (18.5cm) long.

26 Begin to attach the pieces

Coil the frame for ⅝in (1.5cm) (approximately 22-25 coils) both ends. Cut two more 25in (63.5cm) lengths of 24-gauge wire. Attach them to each uncoiled end of the frame and coil for ½in (1cm).

27 Hold the double spiral in position, so that the flat edge is against the side that has ½in (1cm) of coils and bind in place 10 times. Coil the frame three times to secure.

Tip: Once you start binding, do not let go until that section is complete, as the wire will loosen and it will be difficult to tighten again.

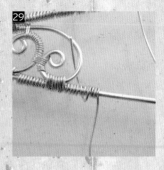

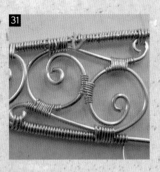

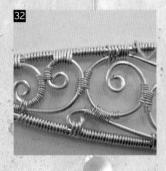

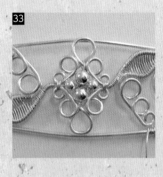

28 Bind the curve of both spirals to the frame seven times, coiling nine times between them. Repeat on the other end. Flatten the binding with the nylon-jaw pliers, locking them in place.

29 You will need to attach a new wire either end. Cut two 25in (63.5cm) of 24-gauge wire and lock it in position between the existing coils, ensuring you trim the ends so that they are hidden on the inside of the cuff.

30 Attach the yin and yang spirals
Lay the spirals inside the frame to check that they fit. The loops and edge of both spirals should touch the frame. If they do not, turn the small loops outwards, using the round-nose pliers until they do.

31 Secure the spirals in position by binding each loop three times and the edge of the spirals seven times, coiling 22 times between them.

32 Once the spirals are attached, secure the yin and yang spirals to the double spirals, by cutting a 10in (25cm) length of 28-gauge wire, coiling the double spiral three times, just before it meets the yin and yang spiral, binding them together five times, then coiling the yin and yang spiral three times to secure. Trim and tuck the ends in.

Repeat on the other end of the cuff.

33 Secure the central detail
Lay the central detail inside the frame, checking with the tape measure that it is perfectly central.
Note: It may be necessary to pull the frame outwards slightly, so that it fits.

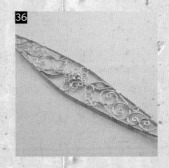

34 Bind both loops three times, securing it in place. Coil eight times, until you reach the leaf on the opposite side. Bind the leaf once and continue coiling until the wire runs out.
Tip: You may need to push a pin through the tip of the leaf, to open the hole, allowing the 24-gauge wire to pass through.

35 Return to the 24-gauge wire left from attaching the loops, coil 30 times. Bind the central loop seven times. Continue coiling until you reach the end of the wire from attaching the leaf, coil three times, and intertwine the two wires, locking them in position. Trim and tuck in. Repeat on the other side.

36 Trim all wire ends
Working your way along the bangle, trim all the wire ends and tuck in on the inside of the frame. Check all the loops are still closed and squeeze all bindings flat with the nylon-jaw pliers.

37 Shape the bangle
Carefully shape the bangle around the mandrel, by pressing it into position with your fingers, working from the centre outwards and taking care to shape the central detail as well as the frame.

38 Once you have the rough shape, use the rawhide mallet to obtain a smooth and even shape. Work methodically around the bangle, using lots of little taps, taking care to avoid the beads so as not to flatten them. Remember to turn the bangle the other way round on the mandrel, so that you work both sides on the same point, allowing for its taper. You will find that the metal hardens as you work.

39 Final step
Once it is shaped, check all wire ends are still tucked in and adjust if necessary.

Variation
Add beads in the open spaces for a more ornate look.

POSEIDON
UNDER-THE-SEA PENDANT

This freeform setting allows you to capture any flat cabochon, stone or shell with a whimsical, swirling wire detail.

This project uses many of the techniques you have learnt earlier in the book, particularly from *Butterfly wing* earrings (see page 57), *Orbital* pendant (see page 65) and *Fern frond* necklace (see page 95).

Note: The measurements of wire given are based on a stone with a 6in (15cm) circumference.

Materials
- 10in (25cm) 18-gauge half-hard round wire
- 25½in (65cm) 20-gauge soft or half-hard round wire
- 140in (3.56m) 28-gauge soft or half-hard round wire
- One flat cabochon, stone or shell (preferably with 6in/15cm circumference)
- Five ⅛in (3mm) round beads
- Six ³/₃₂in (2.5mm) round beads
- Five ¹/₁₆in (2mm) round beads

Tools
- Chain-nose pliers
- Round-nose pliers
- Flat-nose pliers
- Nylon-jaw pliers
- Wire cutters
- ⅛in (3mm) diameter mandrel (kebab stick, knitting needle, wooden dowel, etc)
- Marker pen
- Pin/needle
- Tape measure or ruler and string

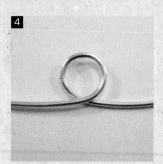

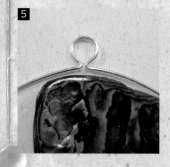

1 Select your stone
This design works best with flat, unusually shaped stones. Although it is possible to set curved stones using this technique (see the ammonite variation at the end of the project), I recommend using a stone that is no more than ¼in (5mm) thick for your first attempt.

2 Once you have chosen your stone, decide on its orientation.

3 Prepare the frame
To calculate the length of wire required for the frame, measure the circumference of the stone (in this case 6in/15cm) then add:
Two x 1½in (4cm) for the spirals on each end of the wire + 1in (2.5cm) for the top loop = 10in (25.5cm) in total. Cut a piece of 18-gauge wire to your required length.
Tip: To measure the stone, you can either use a tape measure, carefully wrapping it around the outside edge of the stone, or if you don't have one, use a piece of string to wrap around the stone and then measure this against a ruler.

4 Form a large loop in the centre of the wire, using the thickest part of the jaws of your round-nose pliers. This will be the loop that the bail is attached to.

5 Carefully bend the straight wires away from each other at the point they cross, using the chain-nose pliers, so that the wire mirrors the shape of your stone at the point you want your bail to be.

6 Now continue shaping the wire, by holding it against the stone and bending the wire around it. The frame should be fractionally larger than the stone to allow for the 28-gauge wire to be coiled around the frame.

7 Remove the wire frame from around the stone and ensure it exactly matches the shape of the stone, as it is very difficult to go back and change it once you have started!

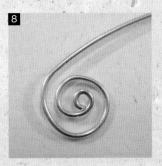

Position of frame spirals

8 Begin the spiral wire detail

The frame wire is finished with a spiral in each end of the wire. In order to know where to position these spirals exactly, you need to first plan and position the rest of the spiral detail. For the stone to be set securely, the bezel decoration needs to cover at least two-thirds of the frame wire, so in this case you need 4in (10cm). The frame spirals will measure approximately ½in (1cm) long once formed, so you need to make 3½in (9cm) of spiral detail in preparation. For larger pendants three sections of spirals are required, for smaller ones (4in/10cm circumference and under) only two sections are needed.

9 Cut three pieces of 20-gauge wire to the following lengths: 6in (15cm); 4½in (12cm); and 3in (7.5cm). Using the 6in (15cm) piece, form an open spiral using the chain-nose pliers. In the straight wire, just after the first spiral, form a second open spiral, in the opposite direction to the first, by first forming a loop and then using the chain-nose pliers to space the wire.

10 Form loops, decreasing gradually in size, until you have used all the wire.

11 Repeat in the other two pieces of wire, forming a single spiral and finishing the wire with loops.
Tip: Try to allow the loops to form interesting shapes.

12 Plan the position of the spirals

Lay the spiral shapes on your stone, ensuring you have as many points of contact with the frame wire as possible. It may be necessary to adjust the shape of the spirals.
Note: Take into account the two frame spirals and leave room for them.
Tip: Try to avoid having the loops in straight lines; add more design interest by shaping them around corners and curves of the stone. This will also add strength to the finished piece and stop the spirals being able to move in their setting.

13 Once you are happy with the position, flatten the spirals with the nylon-jaw pliers. Mark the contact points on your frame wire with a marker pen; this makes it easier when you come to securing it all together.
Tip: Set the spiral details aside, keeping them in their positions to avoid confusion later.

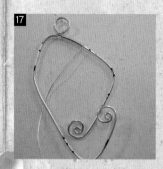

14 Form the frame spirals

Now you have planned the positioning of the decoration, you can form the spirals in the frame wire. Position them so that they sit neatly next to each other or overlap slightly. Trim the straight wires to 1½in (4cm) from the point they cross each other, form a round loop and then spiral, ensuring the frame overlaps slightly before the spirals (these wires will be bound together later).

15 Prepare the spirals for the back

The stone is held in place at the back with two 'S' spirals (you can use more than two if you want to make the back more decorative). Cut two pieces of 20-gauge wire 3½in (9cm) long and form two large 'S' spirals. Lay them on the back of your stone to check they fit. You can adjust their size by tightening or loosening the spirals. The spirals need to be positioned above and below the widest point of the stone, so that it is locked in position and unable to slide out.

16 Once you have achieved the required size, bind the spirals closed with 10in (25cm) 28-gauge wire, as for *Butterfly wing* earrings (see page 57). Position the 'S' spirals on the back of the stone and mark the contact points on the frame wire.

17 Begin construction

Now we begin to connect all the components together. Cut a piece of 28-gauge wire 30in (76cm) long. Attach it to the right of the top loop of the frame wire, by coiling three times, leaving a 1in (2.5cm) tail. Bind the loop closed three times and then begin coiling the frame, until you reach the first pen mark. Binding the loop closed will pull the frame out of line, but this will be rectified when the frame spirals are bound together.

18 Attach the first component

The first pen mark on my frame is for one of the spirals on the back. Hold the spiral in place, on top of the frame (if you are working on the back, like me, remember to turn the frame over, so the spiral is attached to the correct side). Bind the spiral in place nine times, to ensure that it is securely attached. Notice how you are still able to move the spiral up and down; this will allow you to slide the stone into position later.

19 Attach the next embellishment

Continue coiling until you reach the next pen mark. Position your spirals and bind in place.

20 Continue working in this way, coiling until you reach the next pen mark, then binding the loop or spiral in place, ensuring it is sitting on top of the frame wire. Bind as many times as you have room for, as this will make the whole structure much stronger.

21 Add beads
To add more detail and increase the strength of the setting, add beads to fill in gaps and secure the spirals closed. Use the same techniques as in the *Butterfly wing* earrings (see page 57) and *Crescent* ring (see page 83), to secure the beads in position. Use beads of graduating sizes.
Tip: To ensure that the beads are secure and unable to move, make sure that each bead has at least two passes of 28-gauge wire through it and the wire is pulled tightly, locking it in place.

22 Attaching a new wire
Whenever you run out of 28-gauge wire, trim on the inside of the frame and tuck the end in. Cut another 30in (76cm) length of 28-gauge wire. Lock the new wire into the existing coils, ensuring you are coiling in the same direction. This stops the coils from separating and hides the join.

23 Close the frame
Continue coiling and binding, securing your various components in place as you go, until you reach the two frame spirals. Insert your stone to check it fits and position your frame spirals.

24 Once you are happy with them, bind the overlap with the 28-gauge wire to secure in place.

25 Secure the stone in place
Keep working your way around the frame until you reach the point where you need to secure one of the back 'S' spirals closed.

26 Turn the frame upside down, so that you are working on the back and position your stone in place.

27 Bend the spiral over the back of the stone (taking care not to distort the shape of your frame) and bind it in place to the frame. The stone is still able to move in the setting at this point.

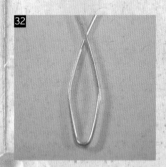

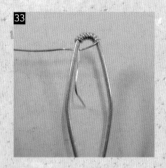

28 Continue working round the frame

Carry on working around your frame, attaching all decorative detail and securing the second back 'S' spiral in place, locking the stone firmly in position.

29 Once you reach the loop at the top of the frame, coil three times to secure, trim and tuck the end in. Trim and tuck in any tails. The wirework should now be rigid. Set aside.

30 Form a bail

Now the pendant is complete, we need to make a bail. Using a 5in (13cm) piece of 20-gauge wire, form a half loop (bent halfway around the jaw of the pliers rather than all the way round) in the centre, using the round-nose pliers, so that the loop is wide enough for two pieces of 20-gauge wire to pass through it.

31 Measure ½in (1cm) along the straight wires and grasp with the thickest part of the jaw on your round-nose pliers.
Tip: You may need to open the loop slightly to fit the pliers in.

32 Bend the wires round the jaws of the pliers, so that they cross over each other, forming a smooth diamond shape, which is 1in (2.5cm) long and ¼in (5mm) at its widest point.

33 Weave the bail

Cut a piece of 28-gauge wire 30in (76cm) long and attach it to the loop by coiling eight times (around the curve) leaving a 1in (2.5cm) tail.

34 Once the thin wire is secured, weave the bail in the same way as you did for the *Orbital* woven round pendant (see page 65) – over, under, coil once.
Tip: When you reach the point where the bail begins to narrow, the weaving wire will have a tendency to slide down the structure wires, leaving gaps in the weave. To stop this from happening, hold the weave in position with your thumbnail, keeping it tight and neat.

Variation

It is possible to set unevenly shaped stones with this method. The stone needs to have a flat or gently domed face. Bend the back spirals to fit the shape of the stone as shown below with this ammonite pendant.

35 Shape the bail

Bend the bail around your ⅛in (3mm) mandrel so that the widest point of the bail is at the top.

36 Thread the pendant onto the straight wires, and then pass the wires through the loop at the top of the bail. Hold the ⅛in (3mm) mandrel in place to shape the bail and pull the wires through the loop, closing the bail. Use the chain-nose pliers to help you pull the wires.

37 Finish the bail

Bend one wire straight up the front of the bail and one straight up the back. Bind the back wire to the back of the bail (just before the weaving starts) three times to secure, coil the nearest thick wire three times and trim.
Tip: The wires may need straightening after shaping the bail.

38 Final step

Trim the 20-gauge wires to 1in (2.5cm) and form a spiral. Position the spirals so that they sit in the centre of the bail front and back.

ECLIPSE

SCALLOPED-EDGE BEZEL

This versatile method of capturing an undrilled stone
in wire can be used for almost any shape, but works best
with circular and oval cabochon.

Instead of using spirals as a decorative detail – as with
all the previous projects, in this design they are the main
structure and it is the repetitive nature of the bezel that
gives a chic look to this reversible pendant.

Although one spiral alone is not that strong, when attached
together, they become very sturdy.

*The materials below are based on a cabochon $^5/_8$ x $^1/_2$ in
(1.5 x 1cm).*

Materials
- 12in (30cm) 20-gauge
  soft or half-hard round
  wire
- 60in (1.52m) 28-gauge
  soft or half-hard round
  wire
- One cabochon $^5/_8$ x $^1/_2$ in
  (1.5 x 1cm)

Tools
- Chain-nose pliers
- Round-nose pliers
- Flat-nose pliers
- Nylon-jaw pliers
- Wire cutters
- $^1/_8$in (3mm) diameter
  mandrel (kebab stick,
  knitting needle, wooden
  dowel, etc)
- Pin/needle
- Tape measure

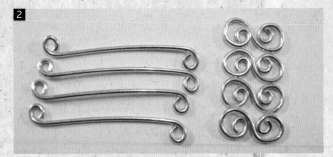

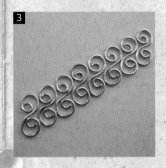

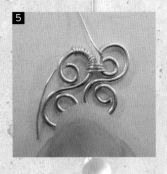

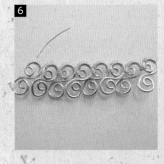

1 Selecting your stone and wire

The bezel is made by securing multiple spirals together to form a flexible strip, which is then secured around the stone and shaped to match its contours.

It is important to select the correct wire gauge for the size stone you are using. If you use a wire that is too thick with a small stone the spirals will be too large and will swamp the stone. If you choose a wire that is too thin with a larger stone you will compromise the strength of the setting.

Below are some guidelines:

Stone circumference	Wire gauge
Under 1½in (4cm)	24
1½in (4cm) to 3¼in (8cm)	20
Over 3¼in (8cm)	18

2 Prepare the spirals

Having selected the stone and wire gauge you will be using, prepare the spirals. Measure the circumference of your stone (in this case 2in/5cm) so using 20-gauge spirals that are ¼in (6mm) wide equates to eight spirals. Therefore cut eight pieces of 20-gauge wire 1½in (4cm) long. Make a round loop in opposite directions at each end and form 'S' spirals (see *Boudica* spirals bracelet, page 103).

3 Begin to connect together

Once you have formed the spirals, lay them together so that the bottom spiral sits in the join of the previous 'S' spiral as shown, making a solid strip that locks together when connected.

Tip: Ensure that the neatest spiral of each 'S' is on the same side, as this edge will be used for the front of the pendant.

4 Cut 25in (63.5cm) of 28-gauge wire. Attach it to the top of one spiral by coiling three times, leaving a 1in (2.5cm) tail.

5 Secure two spirals together

Continue coiling the spiral until you reach the point where the second spiral touches. Bind the second spiral in position three times, ensuring you bind through the loop. Take the 28-gauge wire round the second spiral.

6 Connect all the spirals together

Continue working this way until the top edges of all the spirals are secured together. Once you reach the last spiral, coil, but do not join the bezel together yet. The bezel will not sit flat at this point.

Tip: Ensure you coil each spiral the same amount, as this makes your spacing even and will give you a neat finish. I have coiled each one 12 times.

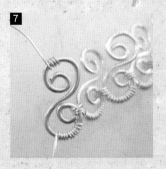
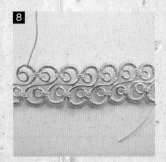

7 Secure the bottom edge
Cut another 25in (63.5cm) of 28-gauge wire. Attach it to the bottom edge of the first spiral by coiling three times, leaving a 1in (2.5cm) tail.

8 Continue working in the same way that you did for the top edge, coiling 12 times and binding three times until the bottom edge is secured in place.
Note: The bezel wire should be strong and flexible now but it won't fit around the stone in its current shape.

9 Shape the bezel
In preparation for setting the stone, the bezel wire needs to be shaped so that it encases the stone. Carefully bend each spiral, by grasping one half in the end of the nylon-jaw pliers and bending by 90° over the jaw.

10 Work your way along the bezel wire until all the spirals have been shaped.
Note: This will cause the wire to curve, which will make it easier to shape and fit around the stone.

11 Secure the stone in place
With the bezel wire shaped, the stone can be set in place. Trim the 1in (2.5cm) tails and tuck the ends in on the inside of the bezel. Hold the stone in place and wrap the bezel around it, ensuring the stone is level in the setting.

12 Squeeze the bezel closed in your fingers and secure in place by binding as before.

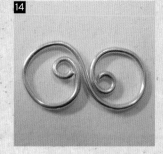

13 Finish shaping the bezel
Trim the 28-gauge wire front and back and tuck the ends in. Now check that your bezel is even and the stone is level in its setting. Use nylon-jaw pliers to push the spirals against the stone.

14 Form a bail
The bail is made in two parts. Firstly make a large 'S' spiral to mirror the bezel pattern, using 2½in (6cm) of 20-gauge wire. Make sure that the outer loops are large enough for the end of your chain to be able to fit through.

15 Bend the 'S' spiral in half and make sure that the two loops line up at the bottom and there is ⅛in (3mm) gap at the top. Adjust if necessary.

16 Attach the bail
Cut 10in (25cm) of 28-gauge wire and attach it to the right of the first bezel spiral you want the bail to be attached to, by coiling three times.

17 Bring the wire through the loop of the 'S' spiral. Thread the 'S' spiral bail onto the wire, making sure the 28-gauge wire passes through both loops. Position the ⅛in (3mm) mandrel above the centre of the two bezel spirals where the bail is to be formed. Take the 28-gauge wire over the mandrel and through the two loops of the second bezel spiral.

Variation

For larger, heavier stones, you can make the bezel even more solid, by binding the loops of the spirals to the side of the spiral when forming the bezel wire. Instead of forming a wrapped connector to attach the bail, make a loop using 1½in (4cm) of 20-gauge wire and attach this directly to the bezel with a round loop on each end.

18 Repeat three times, so that you have four passes of the 28-gauge wire.

19 Coil the four wires together with the 28-gauge wire, creating a wrapped connector. Once you reach the other side of the bail, coil the 'S' spiral three times and trim. Trim the 1in (2.5cm) tail and tuck the ends in.
Tip: Slide the 'S' bail to the opposite side from the one you are working on.

20 Final step
Check the bail is central and straighten. Thread the pendant onto your chain.

GORGON
LAYERED WOVEN PENDANT

This project combines and develops techniques used in the *Mermaid's purse* earrings (see page 73) and the *Orbital* pendant (see page 65). It also shows you how to layer multiple structure wires and intertwine them, locking the wires together to add depth to the design.

Contrast in the wire is created by using both weaving and exposed 18-gauge wire, giving the pendant an ethnic look.

The construction of this pendant, with its multiple frames, was inspired by artist Eni Oken's woven hearts pendant.

Materials
- 1¼in (3cm) 16-gauge soft or half-hard round wire
- 18in (46cm) 18-gauge soft round wire
- 100in (2.54m) 28-gauge soft or half-hard round wire
- One ⁵⁄₈in (1.5cm) flat pear drop, side-drilled bead

Tools
- Chain-nose pliers
- Round-nose pliers
- Flat-nose pliers
- Nylon-jaw pliers
- Wire cutters
- Ring mandrel
- Pin/needle
- Marker pen
- Tape measure

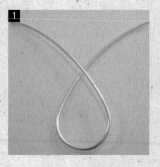
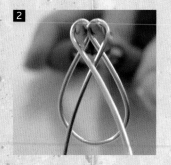
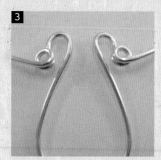

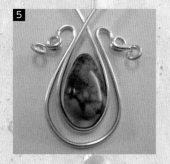
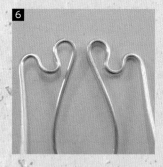

1 **Prepare the outer frame**
Cut a piece of 18-gauge wire 5in (13cm) long and straighten it. Shape the centre of the wire around the ring mandrel, UK size F (US 3¼), creating a drop shape, with the straight wires measuring just over 1¼in (3cm).

2 Grasp the crossover of the wire with the round-nose pliers and bend the wires round and downwards, ensuring both loops are the same size and that you are left with straight wires that are 1in (2.5cm) long.

3 Form a complete circle either side, so that the wire is doubled at the bottom of the loop, by grasping the outer, straight edge of the loop with the round-nose pliers and wrapping around the jaw one-and-a-half times.

4 Trim the straight wires to ¼in (5mm) and form a round loop, creating a figure-of-eight with the double loop. Bend the round loop upwards by 45°. Set aside.

5 **Shape the inner frame**
Cut a piece of 18-gauge wire 7in (18cm) long and straighten. Shape the centre around the ring mandrel UK size B (US size 1). Check that your drop fits inside this frame (allow room for the 28-gauge wire to pass between the stone and frame). Also check that the inner frame fits inside the outer frame.

6 Form three half loops using the round-nose pliers. Work both sides at the same time to ensure they are symmetrical. Ensure you have at least 1¾in (4.5cm) of straight wire left either side. **Tip:** Allow the straight wires to bend upwards in preparation for securing the two frames together.

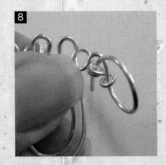

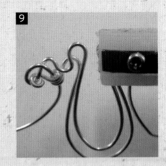

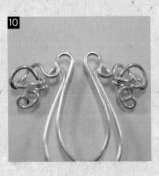

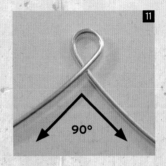

90°

7 **Attach the two frames together**
Slide the straight wires of the inner frame through the round loops of the outer frame.

8 Hold in position with your less dominant hand and bend the straight wires round, passing them to the back, through the double loop.
Tip: You may need to use the chain-nose pliers to help you pull the wire through the loops, as the wire will be getting work hardened by now and increasingly difficult to manipulate.

9 Once you have threaded the wires through the loops on both sides, check they are even and that you have a nice smooth curve. Flatten the inter-looped sections into position on both sides with the nylon-jaw pliers.

10 Form two round loops in both straight wires, so that the wire detail tapers off smoothly.

11 **Form the top loops**
Now the main frame is shaped, prepare the top loops. Cut a piece of 18-gauge wire 3in (7.5cm) long. Form a large loop in the centre of the wire, so that the straight wires form a 90° angle.

12 Form two more round loops on either side, decreasing in size, following the instructions of the *Fern frond* necklace steps 5, 6 and 7 (see page 96), using the round-nose pliers. Flatten with the nylon-jaw pliers. Set aside.

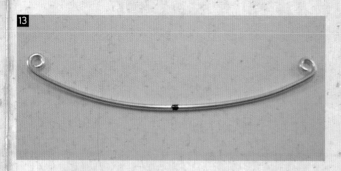 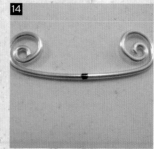 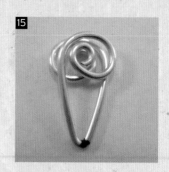

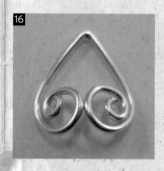 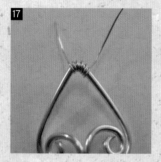  

13 Shape the heart frame
Cut another piece of 18-gauge wire 3in (7.5cm) long. Mark the centre of the wire with a marker pen. Form a round loop at each end.

14 Form an open spiral, using the chain-nose pliers to space the wire, for one turn.

15 Use the flat-nose pliers to bend the wire in half at the pen mark, so that the two spirals overlap.

16 Open the heart so the spirals meet in the centre. Bend the spirals upwards by 30° each, to give the impression the heart is curved and also so that it fits around the stone. Turn the heart upside down; this is the position it will be secured to the frame in. Notice how the sharp bend in the centre has created a nice point to the heart.

17 Weave the heart
Cut a piece of 28-gauge wire 25in (63.5cm) long and attach it to the point of the heart by coiling six times.

18 Take the wire over one side of the frame and under the opposite side, coil once, pulling tightly to secure.

19 Continue weaving in the same way as you did for the *Orbital* pendant (see page 65) – over, under and coil once – until you reach the spirals. Coil the nearest thick wire three times to secure. Do not trim the length of wire, only its 1in (2.5cm) tail. Set aside.

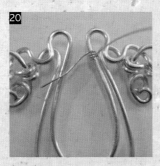

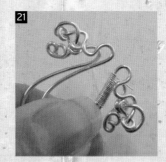

20 Bind the main frame
Although the two main frames are attached together, they are still able to move. To secure them in position before weaving the bottom, the sides need to be bound together. Cut two pieces of 28-gauge wire 15in (38cm) long. Attach one length to the right hand side of the inner frame, just above the point where the two frames run parallel to each other, by coiling three times.

21 Bind the two frame wires together, taking care that the binding is tight and straight. Bind the frame for ½in (1cm), and then coil the inner frame three times to secure, trim and tuck in. Notice how the frame has been pulled slightly out of line.

22 Repeat on the left side with the second piece of 28-gauge wire, taking care to pull the frame back into line. Notice how rigid the frame is now.

23 Weave the frame
Cut a piece of 28-gauge wire 25in (63.5cm) long and attach it to the outer frame on the right hand side, by coiling three times, leaving a 1in (2.5cm) tail. As the bottom of the frame is curved, it needs to be woven in the same way as the *Ammonite* pendant (see page 111), to allow for this. Pass the 28-gauge wire under the outer frame, over the inner frame, and then back under the inner frame (do not coil the inner frame) and over the outer frame. Coil the outer frame three times.

24 Repeat this, working your way round to the other side. Tip: Once you are over half way, the wire has a tendency to slip round the curve, leaving unsightly gaps. Keep this from happening by holding the wire in position with your index finger of your less dominant hand, while holding the frame with your remaining fingers.

25 Once the weaving is complete, coil the outer frame three times, trim the wire and its 1in (2.5cm) tail and tuck in.

26 Begin to attach all the frames
Now all the weaving is complete, the frames can be attached together. Cut a piece of 28-gauge wire 20in (50cm) long and attach the centre to the two top loops of the main frame, binding them together three times to close the frame.

27 Position the heart and bind the point to the loops behind twice each side, to secure in place.
Tip: You may need to open the space at the point of the heart, by pushing a pin or needle through before attaching to the main frame.

28 Attach the loops
Before securing the loops in place, give them a slight curve, by grasping one side with the nylon-jaw pliers and bending the other half downwards slightly; this should make them sit neatly on the main frame.

29 Bind the medium two loops to the top loops of the inner frame nine times each side, pulling tightly. Notice how this pulls the loops upwards.

30 Bind the small loops to the top loops of the outer frame four times each side. Tip: You will need to really squeeze the loops against the frame while you bind to close the gap as much as possible. Coil the nearest thick wire three times to secure. Keep checking the loops are in line while you are securing them in place.

31 Secure the heart in position
Using the 28-gauge wire left from weaving the heart, bind the heart to the frame through the last complete loop on the side detail three times, pulling this wire detail against the frame. Coil the spiral until you reach the centre of the heart.

32 Bind the centre together three times. Coil the other spiral until you reach the other side and bind the left side of the heart to the frame and loop three times, so that the piece is symmetrical. Coil the nearest thick wire three times to secure, then trim and tuck in.

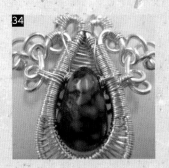

Variation
Add beads instead of weaving the main frame using the techniques learnt from the *Crescent* ring (see page 83) and the *Fern frond* necklace (see page 95).

33 Attach the drop
Using the 28-gauge wire left from attaching the top loops, thread the drop onto both wires, so that they cross over inside the bead.

34 Wrap the wire around the frame once each side, pulling tightly to lock into place between the existing bindings. Coil the wires that pass into the bead each side three times, trim and tuck in. The heart on the front should stop the drop from being able to move.
Tip: It can be tricky passing the wire in such small gaps, so create a small hook in the end of the wire, enabling you to thread the wire that you want to coil.

35 Final step
Carefully shape the side detail by bending downwards with the nylon-jaw pliers to create a curved effect on the front. This also allows the pendant to sit flat now the stone is in place.

36 Add a large tapered figure-of-eight link, made with 1¼in (3cm) of 16-gauge wire, to the top loop.

ORCHID
3D BROOCH

Inspired by orchid flowers, this three-dimensional design is by far the most challenging project in this book. Unlike the real blooms, which are considered very delicate, the finished brooch is surprisingly robust.

Materials
- 15in (38cm) 18-gauge half-hard round wire
- 190in (4.83m) 28-gauge soft or half-hard round wire
- Seven $\frac{1}{8}$in (3mm) or $\frac{3}{16}$in (4mm) round or rondel beads
- One brooch pin

Tools
- Chain-nose pliers
- Round-nose pliers
- Wire cutters
- Flat-nose pliers
- Nylon-jaw pliers
- $\frac{1}{8}$in (3mm) diameter mandrel (kebab stick, knitting needle, wooden dowel, etc)
- Pin/needle
- Tape measure

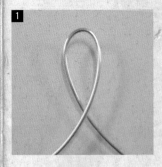
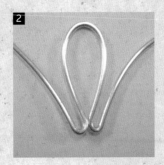
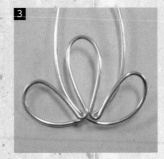
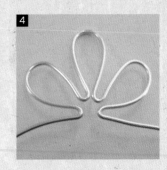
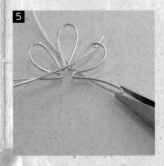
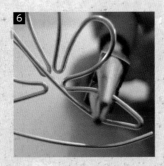
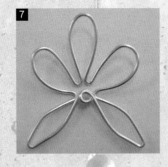

1 Shape the main frame
The flower is constructed from two structure wires. The main one forms all of the petals. This is the one that we will make first. Cut 9in (23cm) of 18-gauge wire and straighten. Form a large loop in the centre that is ³⁄₄in (2cm) tall and ³⁄₈in (9.5mm) wide, by crossing the ends of the wire over and pulling them evenly until you achieve the correct size.

2 Grasp one of the straight wires with the flat-nose pliers at the point it crosses itself and bend upwards by 160°. Repeat on the other side.

3 Form another large loop either side of the first ¹⁄₂in (1cm) long and ³⁄₈in (9.5mm) wide, by pulling the straight wires round with your fingers, ensuring that both petals are the same size and shape.

4 Grasp one of the straight wires with the flat-nose pliers at the point they cross in the centre of the flower and bend outwards by 160°. Repeat on the other straight wire.

5 Form the two bottom petals
The bottom two petals are longer and thinner than the top three, so require more shaping. Measure ³⁄₄in (2cm) along the straight wire and, using the flat-nose pliers, make a sharp 180° bend. Pinch the bend closed with the flat-nose pliers.

6 Open the petal up again with your fingers, creating a pinched tip. Grasp the centre of the petal with the round-nose pliers and bend both the top and bottom wires around the jaw, so that the widest point is ¹⁄₄in (5mm) and the petal is ³⁄₄in (2cm) long.

7 Repeat on the other side. Trim the straight wires to ¹⁄₄in (5mm) from the point they cross and form a round loop in each, so that they sit on top of each other. Flatten with the nylon-jaw pliers.

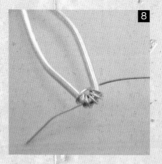

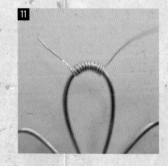

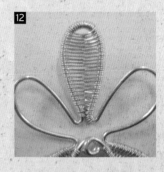

8 Weave the bottom petals
Cut 25in (63.5cm) of
28-gauge wire and attach to
the tip of one of the bottom
petals by coiling six times,
leaving a 1in (2.5cm) tail.
Weave the petal in the same
way as the *Orbital* pendant
(see page 65) – over, under,
coil once.

9 Keep the weave tight and
neat. This will become more
challenging once you are past
the halfway point and the
petal starts to narrow again.
Keep the weave in position,
using your thumbnail as a
stopper against the 28-gauge
wire, while you secure it with
a coil on the opposite side.

10 Once you reach the point
where the structure wires
meet, coil the bottom wire
three times to secure, trim
and tuck the end in. Repeat
on the other bottom petal.

11 Weave the top petal
Cut 25in (63.5cm) of
28-gauge wire and attach
it to the tip of the top petal
by coiling 12 times, to allow
for the curve of the petal,
leaving a 1in (2.5cm) tail.

12 Weave in the same way as
before – over, under, coil once
– until the petal is complete.
Remember to hold the
weaving in position with your
thumbnail. Once the petal is
woven, coil the nearest thick
wire three times to secure,
then trim and tuck the end in.

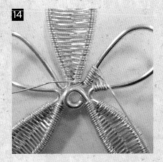

13 Begin work on the side petals

Check that your flower has not become misshapen during the weaving and that the round loops are perfectly central and sit one on top of the other. Adjust if necessary. This time the weaving starts at the other end of the petal, to give more control to the position of the beads.

Cut a 30in (76cm) length of 28-gauge wire and attach it to the upper wire of the right petal, coiling three times, leaving a 1in (2.5cm) tail, just after the bend.

14 Weave as before four times.

15 Attach a bead

Once the 28-gauge wire is back on the top wire of the petal, thread a bead onto the wire. Position the bead so that half of it overlaps the existing weaving.

16 Continue weaving but do not pull too tightly on the first pass of the wire after attaching the bead, as this will pull the weaving out of line. Weave five times. Ensure that the weave sits beneath the bead and that there are no gaps along the structure wire. The bead should still be able to move slightly.

17 Attach two more beads

Secure the second bead in place. Weave another five times and secure the third bead. Weave again five times. This should take you to the tip of the petal.

18 Coil the tip approximately 16 times, (as many times as you can neatly squeeze in) to lock the weaving in place. Tip: Use a pin or needle to open the space between the weave and frame wire, to allow you to coil.

19 Wrap the beads

To secure the beads in place and make them look more attractive, each bead needs to be wrapped. Thread the 28-gauge wire through the weaving to the front, next to the third bead.

Note: The photo shows the back view.

20 Wrap once around the bead, pulling tightly, so that the wrap is not able to pass over the bead.

Tip: If you are not able to get the wrap tight enough, due to the shape of the bead, coil once around the wire that passes through the bead to lock the wire in place.

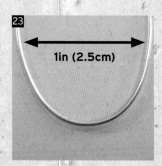

1in (2.5cm)

¹/₂in
(1cm)

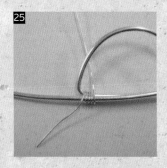

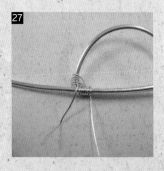

21 Wrap the next two beads in the same way, ensuring the wire is secured in place before moving onto the next bead. Coil the nearest structure wire three times to secure, trim this wire and the 1in (2.5cm) tail and tuck the end in.

22 Repeat steps 13–21 on the other petal, ensuring that the beads are symmetrical. Set aside.

23 Form the central petal
Cut 6in (15cm) of 18-gauge wire and straighten. Form a large U-shape that is 1in (2.5cm) wide.

24 Measure ¹/₂in (1cm) from the tip of the U, along one of the straight wires, grasp with the flat nose pliers and bend inwards by 90°. Repeat on the other straight wire to form a D shape that is ¹/₂in (1cm) tall and ⁷/₈in (2.2cm) wide, with the straight edge two wires thick.

25 Weave the central petal
Cut a 40in (1.02m) length of 28-gauge wire. Attach it to the flat edge by coiling the left side four times, leaving a 1in (2.5cm) tail. Make sure the coils are very tight so that the two structure wires are locked together.

26 As you pull the wire through, insert a couple of fingers from your less dominant hand into the loop created, to prevent the wire from kinking. As you get further around the shape it will become easier as the length of wire becomes shorter.

27 Begin to weave by passing the 28-gauge wire over the straight edge and under the left side of the curved edge. Coil the curved edge four times. Bring the wire back, by passing it over the curved wire, under the two straight wires and coiling twice.

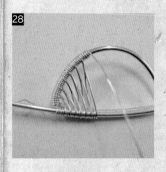

28 Continue weaving
Keep weaving in this way: over, under and coil the curved edge four times; then over, under, coil the straight edge two times. This allows for the curve of the shape.

29 Continue until you have completed the shape. Once you reach the end, coil the flat edge four times to secure. Do not trim.

30 Shape the central petal
Hold your 1/8in (3mm) mandrel in the centre of the straight edge of the D shape and fold the petal around it, so that the straight wires are pointing straight upwards and parallel to each other.

31 Grasp the curved edge with the nylon-jaw pliers and bend it downwards. Work your way carefully around this edge, creating a lip.

32 Attach a bead where the edges of the D shape meet, using the 28-gauge wire left over from the weaving, so that it sits inside the shape. Coil the nearest thick wire three times to secure, trim and tuck the end in. Trim the 1in (2.5cm) tail too.

33 Begin to assemble the flower
Using the flat-nose pliers, bend the two straight wires backwards by 90°.
Note: The photo shows the side view.

34 Thread the straight wires through the gap between the side petals and top petal, ensuring that the central petal is straight.

35 Thread the brooch pin onto the two straight wires on the back, so that it is hidden behind the two side petals from the front.
Note: The photo shows the back view.

36 Secure in place

Thread one straight wire through the two round loops on the flower and the other through the curve of the D shape, to the front of the flower. Pull them tight, locking everything into place.
Tip: The wire will be quite stiff, so use the chain-nose pliers to help you pull the wire through.

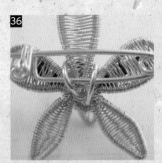

37 Secure the pin in place

Although the pin is now attached, it is still able to move. To secure it in position, cut 14in (35.5cm) of 28-gauge wire and attach the centre of this wire to the centre of the back pin. Coil until you reach the 18-gauge wires, bind the pin to these wires three times either side. Continue coiling until you reach the round loop and spring on either end of the pin. Bind these to the side petals three times. Coil the pin three times to secure the wire, trim and tuck both ends in.

38 Finish shaping

Trim the two straight wires to 1/4in (5mm) from the edge of the central petal and form a round loop in each, to signify the stamen. Bend the top and bottom two petals forward using your fingers.

39 Final step

Grasp the tip of the petals with the nylon-jaw pliers and bend back to add shape. Check everything is central and straight.
Note: The pin wire you can see will be hidden when attached to clothing.

Variation

Instead of a brooch, make a pendant by forming a wrapped connector between the two stamen wires at the back, with a double spiral bail. See *Eclipse* bezel (see page 143) for instructions. Also try experimenting with the shape of the petals - this one has more rounded petals.

THE VINE
PENDANT

This project looks at developing a design.
The main instruction is for a pendant, which has
two contrasting weaves, one for the leaves of the
vine and one for the bail. It also shows a more ornate
way of wrapping a briolette, as well as using techniques
you have already learnt earlier in the book.

Once you have mastered the basics of this design, you can
move on to some variations and look at how to develop a
design into a collection of jewelry.

Materials
- 12in (30cm) 18-gauge soft or half-hard round wire
- 17in (43cm) 20-gauge soft round wire
- 4in (10cm) 20- or 24-gauge soft or half-hard round wire (for bead dangles)
- 114in (2.9m) 28-gauge soft or half-hard round wire
- 10–15 x ⅛in (3mm), ³⁄₁₆in (4mm) or ⁵⁄₁₆in (6mm) round or rondel beads
- One or two briolettes

Tools
- Chain-nose pliers
- Round-nose pliers
- Flat-nose pliers
- Nylon-jaw pliers
- Wire cutters
- ⅛in (3mm) diameter mandrel (kebab stick, knitting needle, wooden dowel, etc)
- Masking tape/low tack tape
- Tape measure

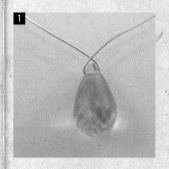

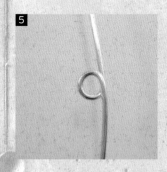

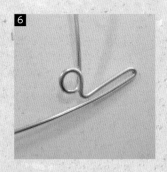

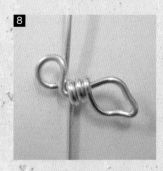

1 Preparation

The first thing to do is make the dangles. For the briolette, cut a piece of 28-gauge wire 10in (25cm) long and thread the briolette 3in (7.5cm) along the wire. Bend both ends of your wire 135° upwards, so that they cross over the bead.

2 Grasp the 3in (7.5cm) wire with the round-nose pliers and wrap the wire twice around the jaw of the pliers, forming a double loop.

3 Wrap the long wire carefully around the briolette, working your way down the bead, ensuring each wrap is neat and tight. Work your way down the bead until you are just past the hole, then bring the wire back up to the top, just below the loop. Wrap twice below the loop to secure.

Tip: Do not let go of the wire whilst you are wrapping as the wire will loosen. You may find it easier to turn the briolette, holding the wire still, as this gives you more control.

4 Wrap the two loops together as you would with a wrapped connector (see *Eclipse* bezel steps 16–19, page 146). Coil the tail of the 3in (7.5cm) wire around the loop three times to secure, trim both wires and tuck the ends in. Make four bead dangles, using either 20- or 24-gauge wire, depending on the size of your bead holes. Set aside.

5 Prepare the main frame wire

The main frame wire runs down the centre of the pendant and shapes the leaves. Cut a piece of 18-gauge wire 12in (30cm) long and straighten. Measure 3in (7.5cm) from one end and form a round loop, so that the wire either side forms a straight line.

6 Just after the loop, make a 120° bend in the opposite direction to the loop. Measure ½in (1cm) from this bend and make a sharp 180° bend. Using the flat-nose pliers, pinch the bend closed.

7 Use the round-nose pliers to help you open the bend again, creating a pinched tip. Then bend your wire either side of the bend around the jaw of the pliers, forming a leaf shape just over ¼in (5mm) long.

8 Wrap the leaf closed three times, ensuring the straight wire points downwards, continuing in line with the 3in (7.5cm) wire at the top.

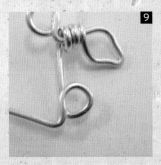

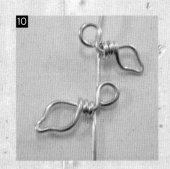

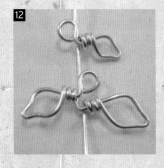

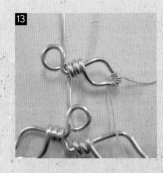

9 Form a second loop and leaf

Measure ¼in (5mm) from the first leaf and form a second loop in the same direction as the leaf.

10 Using the flat-nose pliers make a 120° bend in the opposite direction. Measure ⅝in (1.5cm) from the bend and form a second leaf shape, slightly larger than the first and on the opposite side of the frame.

11 Form a third leaf

Just after the second leaf, make a 120° bend in the opposite direction. Measure ¾in (2cm) from this bend and make a sharp 180° bend.

12 Shape the third leaf and wrap three times to close. Check that the wire between each leaf forms a straight line.

13 Weave the leaves

To finish the leaves, they need to be woven. Cut a piece of 28-gauge wire 20in (50cm) long and attach it to the tip of the smallest leaf, by coiling three times, leaving a 1in (2.5cm) tail. Weave as you did for the *Orbital* pendant (see page 65) - over, under, coil once.

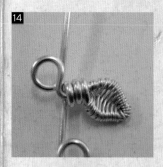

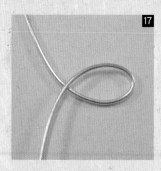

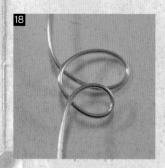

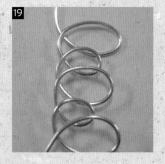

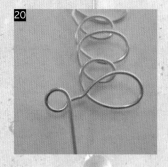

14 Keep going until you reach the other end. Coil three times to secure. Trim and tuck the wire and its 1in (2.5cm) tail.

15 Reattach the 28-gauge wire to the next leaf and weave. Then weave the third leaf with a piece of 28-gauge wire 14in (35.5cm) long.

16 Form a wrapped loop
Measure ¼in (5mm) from the bottom leaf, make a 90° bend, then form a loop. Thread a briolette and two dangles onto the loop and wrap closed three times. The whole piece should now measure 1 ⅛in (2.8cm) from the top loop to the bottom one. Set aside.

17 Prepare the second structure wire
This second wire forms the loops and creates the vine effect. Cut a piece of 20-gauge wire 17in (43cm) long and straighten. Measure 3in (7.5cm) from one end and form a loop by crossing the long end of the wire over the short end and pulling until the loop is ½in (1cm) tall.

18 Form a second loop, by crossing the long wire over the end of the first loop and pulling, creating a loop that is ¼in (5mm) tall.

19 Continue in this way, alternating the size of the loops, until you have five in total. The total length of the loops should be 1in (2.5cm). Ensure that the inside of the loops form a straight line. Flatten with the nylon-jaw pliers.
Tip: If you need to reduce the length slightly, you can make the loops overlap.

20 Form a wrapped loop
Using the flat-nose pliers, bend the long straight wire upwards by 45° at the point it crosses the loop. Measure ⅛in (3mm) from this bend, then bend downwards by 45° and form a round loop.

21 Thread a briolette and two dangles (or just dangles if you are only using one briolette) onto the loop and wrap closed three times, bringing the straight wire back to the front.

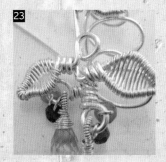

22 Attach the two frames together

Position the leaf frame in place, on top of the loop frame, so that the loops sit to the right of the central line of the leaf frame. Tape the two 3in (7.5cm) straight wires at the top to hold the frames in position.

23 Take the 20-gauge wire from wrapping the loop closed over the central leaf frame, just above the wrapped loop and through the bottom loop on the opposite side, locking the frames together.

24 Form the loops on the left

In order to secure the two frames together and balance the pendant, you need to form loops on the left, working your way back up the pendant. For this next stage, turn the pendant over, so that you are working on the back. Shape a loop, crossing the wire over itself, so it is 1/2in (1cm) tall.

25 Once the loop is shaped, thread the wire over the front of the pendant and through the loop on the opposite side, taking care to avoid the dangles. The wire should sit between the second leaf and loop of the main frame.

26 Form a second loop, 3/8in (9.5mm) tall, threading through the middle loop on the opposite side. Form a third and final loop in the same way. This will create a twisted vine effect.

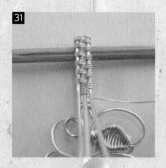

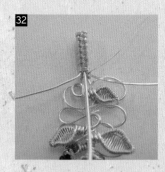

27 Remove the tape and wrap the longest 20-gauge wire (from the right) around the other two straight wires twice, securing them together. Position all three straight wires so that they are pointing straight up, with the 18-gauge wire in the centre. Check they are all parallel and straighten if necessary.

28 Weave the bail
Cut 30in (76cm) of 28-gauge wire. Attach it to one of the outer wires by coiling three times, leaving a 1in (2.5cm) tail. Working on the back of the pendant, bind the outer wire to the central wire three times, ensuring that they are sitting next to each other and do not become bunched up.

29 Take the 28-gauge wire under the outer wire on the opposite side and bind this wire to the central wire three times.

30 Repeat this until you have covered 1in (2.5cm) of the bail wires. Then coil the central wire three times to secure. *Note: The pattern on the front will be different from the weave on the back. Also notice just how strong this weave is.*

31 Shape the bail
Position the mandrel in the centre of the woven section and bend the bail wires over it, forming the bail. Bend the straight wires upwards 45°, using the flat-nose pliers, after the end of the weave.

32 Trim the 1in (2.5cm) tail of the 28-gauge wire and tuck in. Bind the bail closed four times and coil a thick wire three times to secure. Splay the three wires outwards and trim each one to 1½in (4cm) from the binding.

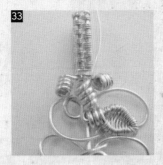

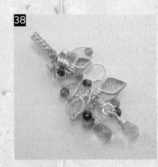

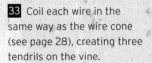

Variations

Experiment with the size of the beads. Notice how larger beads give a fuller look to the design, while smaller beads leave more open space. Create a two-wire bail, by using the 18-gauge wire to wrap the bail wires together three times in step 27 and trimming the wire. Then weave the two 20-gauge wires in the same way as the leaves. You can also experiment with colour combinations.

33 Coil each wire in the same way as the wire cone (see page 28), creating three tendrils on the vine.

34 Thread a bead onto the 28-gauge wire and create a bird's nest setting to secure it in place. Coil the nearest thick wire three times to secure, trim and tuck the end in.

35 Attach the beads
Plan the position of the beads on the pendant.

36 Then cut a piece of 28-gauge wire 20in (50cm) long and attach it to the thick wire where you would like the first bead to be secured, by coiling three times, leaving a 1in (2.5cm) tail. Thread the bead onto the wire and create a bird's nest setting (see page 100) to secure it in place.

37 Move the wire to the next position for a bead by coiling a thick wire or trimming and re-attaching in the correct place. Repeat this until you have attached all the beads. Tip: Wherever possible, use structure wires from loops that are next to each other, so that you lock them together when attaching a bead, further strengthening the pendant.

38 Final step
Adjust the position of the leaves slightly, so that they are angled and check that the main loop is in line with the bail.

THE VINE
EARRINGS

This variation shows you how to make a pair of earrings. The construction of these is different from the other variations, as they are made from a single structure wire and are much more compact, although the basic principles are the same.

The finished earrings have a drop of 1³/₄in (4.5cm) and the wirework measures 1¹/₄in (3cm).

Materials
- 22in (56cm) 20-gauge soft round wire
- 4in (10cm) 20- or 24-gauge soft round wire (depending on the size of your bead holes, for the dangles)
- 71in (1.8m) 28-gauge soft or half-hard round wire
- 20 x ¹/₁₆in (2mm) or ¹/₈in (3mm) round or rondel beads
- Four briolettes
- One pair of coiled earwires

Tools
- Chain-nose pliers
- Round-nose pliers
- Flat-nose pliers
- Nylon-jaw pliers
- Wire cutters
- Tape measure

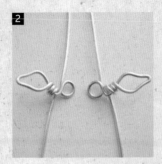

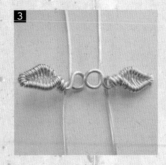

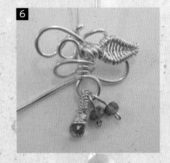

1 Prepare the dangles
Wrap the four briolettes with approximately 10in (25cm) of 28-gauge wire each and form the dangles with 20- or 24-gauge wire (depending on their hole size) following steps 1 to 4 of *The vine* pendant. Set aside.

2 Prepare the frame wires
The vine earrings are made from a single structure wire, making them more compact and therefore more suitable for earrings. Working with 20-gauge wire also makes them lighter. Cut two 11in (28cm) lengths of 20-gauge wire and straighten. Form a single small leaf and loop in each wire, 3in (7.5cm) from one end, following steps 5–8 of *The vine* pendant.
Note: Ensure that they are on opposite sides, so that the earrings are mirror images of each other.
Tip: Work both wires at the same time, making sure you have an identical pair.

3 Weave the leaves using approx 8in (20cm) of 28-gauge wire per leaf, following steps 13 and 14 of *The vine* pendant.

4 Attach some dangles
Form a round loop ⅛in (3mm) below the leaf on each frame. Thread a briolette and two dangles onto each loop and wrap closed three times.

5 Form the loops
In the long length of wire, form one loop ⅓in (8.5mm) tall and one ³⁄₁₆in (4mm) tall on the same side as the leaf on both frames, following steps 17 and 18 of *The vine* pendant. Coil the 3in (7.5cm) wire once to secure.

6 Form two more loops, working your way down the other side of the frame, intertwining with the loops on the opposite side. Ensure both earrings are the same. Flatten with the nylon-jaw pliers.

7 **Form a wrapped loop**
Coil the first loop once to secure the wire in place.

8 Form a round loop ⅛in (3mm) from the loop you just coiled, thread a briolette and two dangles on and wrap closed three times, trim and tuck the end in. Repeat on the other earring.

9 **Form the top loop**
Measure ⅛in (3mm) from the top coil on the 3in (7.5cm) wire and form a wrapped loop. Trim the straight wire to 1½in (4cm) and form the tendril, by coiling around the jaw of the round-nose pliers.

10 Attach the beads
Using 15in (38cm) of 28-gauge wire, attach the beads to the frame, following steps 35–37 of *The vine* pendant (see page 171).
Note: As the beads are so small, you may not be able to wrap each one.

11 **Final step**
Attach the earwires and check the earrings are in line.

THE VINE
DONUT BAIL

This variation shows you how to make a more compact version of the vine, without any dangles. Instead it uses the design to make an ornate bail for a donut bead, which is a great way to show off a stunning stone.

Materials
- 11in (28cm) 18-gauge soft or half-hard round wire
- 13in (33cm) 20-gauge soft round wire
- 65in (1.65m) 28-gauge soft or half-hard round wire
- Eight round beads, use a mixture of $\frac{1}{16}$in (2mm), $\frac{1}{8}$in (3mm) and $\frac{3}{16}$in (4mm)
- One 1in (2.5cm) donut bead

Tools
- Chain-nose pliers
- Round-nose pliers
- Wire cutters
- Flat-nose pliers
- Nylon-jaw pliers
- $\frac{1}{8}$in (3mm) diameter mandrel (kebab stick, knitting needle, wooden dowel, etc)
- Masking or low-tack tape
- Tape measure

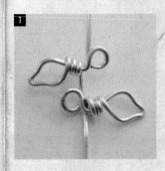 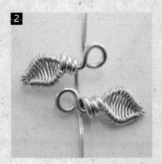 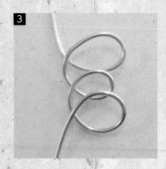 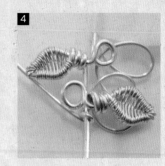

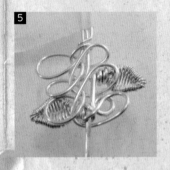  

1 Prepare the main frame
Follow steps 5-10 of *The vine* pendant (see pages 166-167), using 11in (28cm) of 18-gauge wire. Form two leaves and loops, with only 1/8in (3mm) gap between them. This will give you 1/2in (1cm) of shaped frame.

2 Weave the leaves with 20in (50cm) of 28-gauge wire, following steps 13-15 (see pages 167-168) of *The vine* pendant. Set aside.

3 Form a second frame
Cut 13in (33cm) of 20-gauge wire and form three loops, following steps 17-19 of *The vine* pendant (see page 168), the largest loop being 1/3in (8.5mm) tall and the smallest 1/4in (5mm). Leave a 3in (7.5cm) length at the top for the bail. Flatten with nylon-jaw pliers.

4 Secure the two frames together
Position the leaf frame on top of the loop frame and tape the two 3in (7.5cm) bail wires together, to secure them in position. Coil the 20-gauge wire around the 18-gauge once, just below the second leaf, locking the frames together.

5 Follow steps 23-26 of *The Vine* pendant to form three more loops on the opposite side of the frame.

6 Wrap the two bail wires together once with 20-gauge wire. Bend the wire upwards by 45°, so that it is parallel to the other two bail wires and re-tape the three wires together. Flatten with the nylon-jaw pliers. The shaped frame should now be 3/4in (2cm) tall.

7 Attach the beads
As this frame will be attached to the donut, it will be difficult to get to the back of the frame, so the beads need to be attached first. Follow steps 35-37 of *The vine* pendant (see page 171). Using 15in (38cm) of 28-gauge wire, secure all the small beads in place.

8 Attach the donut
Make a 90° bend straight back on the 18-gauge wire just after the last loop at the bottom. Measure ⅛in (3mm) from this bend and bend upwards by 90°.

9 Thread the donut on, so that the leaf detail is sitting on the front of the donut at the top.

10 Secure in place by coiling the 18-gauge wire from the back around the three bail wires three times, trim and then tuck the end in. Remove the tape.

11 Weave and shape the bail
Using 30in (76cm) of 28-gauge wire, weave the bail, following the instructions in steps 28–30 of *The Vine* pendant, remembering to work on the back. Once woven, bend the bail backwards by 45° with the nylon-jaw pliers, so that you don't damage the weave.

12 Shape the bail, using a ⅛in (3mm) mandrel, following steps 31 and 32 of *The vine* pendant (see page 170).

13 Splay the three wires and form the tendrils.

14 Final step
Attach a bead to the front of the bail and wrap three times. Coil the nearest thick wire three times to secure, trim and tuck the end in.

THE VINE
CUFF

This is the most challenging of the Vine variations due to the length of wire you will be working with for the main frame.

It is not for the faint-hearted as there is a lot of work involved, but it is well worth the effort.

Materials
- 42 ¼in (1.07m) of 16-gauge soft round wire
- 63in (1.6m) 18-gauge soft round wire
- 250in (6.35m) 28-gauge soft or half-hard round wire
- 34 x assorted ³⁄₁₆in (4mm), ¼in (5mm) and ⁵⁄₁₆in (6mm) beads

Tools
- Chain-nose pliers
- Round-nose pliers
- Wire cutters
- Flat-nose pliers
- Nylon-jaw pliers
- Hammer
- Anvil
- Bracelet mandrel
- Tape measure

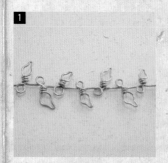

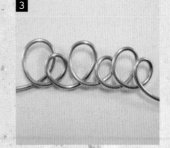

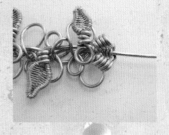

1 Form the leaf frame

Cut 36in (91.5cm) of 16-gauge wire and straighten. Follow steps 5-12 of *The vine* pendant (see pages 166-167) to form the leaves and loops on the frame wire. Continue forming until you have 10 leaves in total alternating in size. You should have 4 1/2in (12cm) of shaped frame wire in total, with 3in (7.5cm) of straight wire at each end.

2 Weave the leaves

Following steps 13-15 of *The vine* pendant (see pages 167-168), weave all the leaves with 28-gauge wire, below is a guide for the amount of wire required:

- Small leaf = 8 1/2in (22cm) wire
- Medium leaf = 12in (30cm) wire
- Large leaf = 13in (33cm) wire.

3 Prepare the second frame wire

Cut a piece of 18-gauge wire 17in (43cm) long and form six loops of alternating sizes, following steps 17-19 of *The vine* pendant (see page 168).

4 Coil the straight wire once to the main leaf frame (see circled area) to secure it in position (instead of forming a wrapped loop as with the pendant).

5 Form the loops on the other side of the frame, following steps 24-26 in *The vine* pendant (see page 169).

6 Secure in place

Once you have formed all your loops on the other side of the frame and you are back at the start, coil the straight wires together with the longest 18-gauge wire, to secure them together. Bend the two 18-gauge wires round to the front of the bracelet, leaving the 16-gauge wire straight.

7 Form two coils in these wires for the vine tendrils.

8 Complete the cuff frame

Cut another piece of 18-gauge wire 17in (43cm) long. Form another six loops as before. Attach it to the opposite side of the frame, with the 3in (7.5cm) straight wire passed to the front of the cuff.

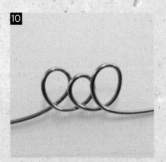

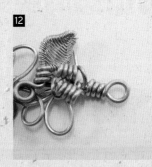

9 Form the loops on the other side and secure the frame in place as before. Once you have attached three 17in (43cm) lengths of 18-gauge wire in total, you will have one leaf and loop set that does not have loops behind it.

10 Cut 12in (30cm) of the 18-gauge wire and form three loops.

11 Attach it to the end of the cuff and work to meet the existing loops, and then back up the other side, forming two coils at the end to match the other side.

12 Form wrapped loops
Measure ¼in (5mm) from the coils on each end and form a large wrapped loop in the 16-gauge wire at both ends. The frame should now measure 6in (15cm) in total.

13 Attach beads
Secure all the beads in place with 28-gauge wire, forming a bird's nest setting (see page 100) around each one. You will use approximately 20in (50cm) for every five beads.

14 Shape the cuff
Once all the beads are secured in place, attach a hook and tapered figure-of-eight clasp, using two figure-of-eight links, all of which are hammered, using the measurements of wire shown below:
- Hook = 2in (5cm) 16-gauge
- Tapered figure-of-eight = 1½in (4cm) 16-gauge
- Two figure-of-eights = 1¼in (3cm) 16-gauge.

15 Final step
Gently shape the cuff around your mandrel, using only your fingers to push everything in to place.

THE VINE
NECKLACE

A highly ornate version of *The vine* design, this necklace is perfect for a special occasion.

You need to be familiar with *The vine* earrings and pendant in order to make this.

Materials
- 23in (58.5cm) 18-gauge soft
  or half-hard round wire
- 51in (1.3m) 20-gauge soft round wire
- 275in (6.9m) 28-gauge soft or half-hard round wire
- 21 x ⅛in (3mm) to ⁵/₁₆in (6mm) round or rondel beads
- 12 briolettes
- 12in (30cm) chain
- One clasp

Tools
- Chain-nose pliers
- Round-nose pliers
- Flat-nose pliers
- Nylon-jaw pliers
- Wire cutters
- ⅛in (3mm) diameter mandrel (kebab stick, knitting needle, wooden dowel, etc)
- Ring mandrel
- Marker pen
- Tape measure

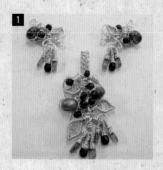

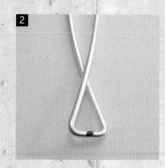

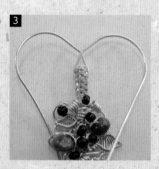

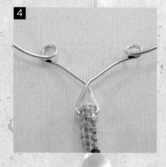

1 Preparation

The necklace is made up from several components, so the first thing to do is prepare these. Make one pendant and a pair of earrings. Do not attach dangles to the final loop at the bottom of each earring, as this will be used to connect them together. Set aside.

2 Form the connector wire

Cut a piece of 18-gauge wire 10in (25cm) long and straighten it. Mark the centre (5in/13cm) with a marker pen. Measure ⅛in (3mm) from this mark on each side and bend upwards by 120°, to form a triangle, which measures ⅜in (9.5mm) tall and ¼in (5mm) wide.

3 Thread the pendant

onto the triangle. Bend the two 18-gauge wires 45° downwards at the point that they cross. Shape the straight wires around the ring mandrel on UK size Q (US size 8), for a third of a circle, immediately after the triangle each side, in order to obtain a smooth downward curve.

4 Form the loops and leaves

Measure ½in (1cm) either side of the triangle and mark with the marker pen. Grasp this point with the round-nose pliers and form a round loop either side, so that it sits above the frame.

5 Form a small leaf either side, just after the loop, in the opposite direction following the instructions in *The vine* pendant steps 5–8 (see page 166).

6 Weave each leaf with a piece of 28-gauge wire 15in (38cm) long. Do not trim the wire. Instead use this wire to attach a bead to the loop, by following the coils of the wrapped leaf. Create a bird's nest setting (see page 100). Coil the nearest thick wire three times to secure, trim and tuck the end in.

7 Attach the side sections Measure ¼in (5mm) from the leaves and bend the straight wire upwards by 45°.

8 Form a round loop that faces front to back rather than top to bottom on one side. Thread the side detail on. Wrap the loop closed three times. Repeat on the other side.

9 **Final step**
Cut two 6in (15cm) lengths of chain and attach to each side with a wrapped link, using 20-gauge wire. Attach a wrapped link to each end of your chain, with one securing the clasp to the necklace.

SHOPPING LIST

MATERIALS USED IN THIS BOOK:

WIRE
- 16-gauge soft and half-hard round
- 18-gauge soft and half-hard round
- 20-gauge soft and half-hard round
- 24-gauge soft and half-hard round
- 28-gauge soft and half-hard round

BEADS AND STONES
- 1/16in (2mm) round beads
- 1/8in (3mm) round beads
- 3/16in (4mm) round beads
- 1/4in (5mm) round beads
- 5/16in (6mm) round beads
- 9/16in (14mm) round beads
- 1/16in (2mm) rondelles
- 1/8in (3mm) rondelles
- 3/16in (4mm) rondelles
- 5/16in (6mm) rondelles
- Semi-precious chips
- 5/8in–3/4in (15-20mm) oval beads
- Briolettes
- 5/8in (15mm) flat pear drop, side drilled
- 1in x 11/16in (25mm x 18mm) oval cabochon
- 5/8in x 1/32in (15mm x 10mm) cabochon
- 1in (25mm) donut bead
- Flat cabochon, stone or shell
  (preferably with 6in/15cm circumference)

METAL BEADS
- 1/16in (2mm) round
- 3/32in (2.5mm) round
- 1/8in (3mm) round
- 3/16in (4mm) round

CHAIN
- Rolo chain
- Hammered oval chain

FINDINGS
- Butterfly earring backs
- Clasps

ONLINE SUPPLIERS

www.bluemud.com
Bluemud for silver wire, chain and beads

www.firemountaingems.com
Fire Mountain Gems a huge selection of all jewelry-making supplies, great for semi-precious beads

www.limabeads.com
Lima Beads great choice of semi precious beads, also has a useful feature for suggested combinations of stones

www.beadsdirect.co.uk
Beads Direct fantastic choice of very reasonably priced semi-precious beads

www.bluestreakbeads.co.uk
Blue Streak Beads supplier of Bali silver beads (among others)

www.pasternakfindings.com
Pasternak Findings competitively priced supplier of silver and gold jewelry findings (including silver wire)

www.wires.co.uk
Wires supplier of wire in just about every metal you can think of. Great for your practice wire!

www.palmermetals.co.uk
Palmer metals wire and tool supplier in the UK

www.cooksongold.com
Cooks on Gold huge selection of jewelry-making equipment and materials, including tools

www.beadworks.co.uk
Beadworks large selection of jewelry supplies

www.boxesandbusts.co.uk
Boxes and Busts for packaging, displays, storage bags and boxes

www.towntalkshop.co.uk
Town Talk polishing and cleaning products

ABOUT THE AUTHOR

Born and raised in North London, Abby grew up surrounded by artistic people. Living in a very close local community with a diverse mix of characters, she was able to try her hand at a whole array of crafts, from sewing to polymer clay modelling.

Abby comes from a long line of artists; her great, great grandfather was Frank Paton, well known for his realistic portrayal of both wild and domestic animals using oil paints, but he is probably more fondly remembered for his etchings. Many other family members have continued the tradition of painting and drawing. Although Abby enjoyed drawing, she wasn't particularly good at it. Imagine her delight when she discovered the possibility of bringing things to life with wire!

Abby's jewelry adventure started when she received a bead weaving loom one Christmas. She started with beadwoven chokers and simple strung necklaces. Then she discovered wire and began making wire wrapped pendants and rosary chains, which have developed into what you see today. The only limitation with wire jewelry-making is your imagination. Abby tends to find her inspiration in the natural world. Whether it is a lifelike replica or an abstract design, she finds this an endless source of ideas.

Abby has found that her jewelry making has got her through many tough times and in 2008 she decided to try and share the pleasure it has given her with others, by offering online tutorials, teaching her designs and the techniques she use. By 2010 she had over 30 online tutorials available and their continued popularity made her realize that it would be really nice to offer a complete, comprehensive guide to wirework in one place - the ideal vehicle, a book!

Abby hopes wirework gives you as much pleasure as it does her!

ACKNOWLEDGEMENTS FROM ABBY

There are so many people who have helped make this book possible, but there are some without whom, I would not have dreamed of writing it. Although you know who you are, everyone else should too, so here goes...

All my family, for making me who I am and keeping me grounded, especially Lesley White, my aunt, for buying me that beading loom all those years ago which started this journey and Margaret Hook, my mum, for always encouraging me to follow my dreams.

Franchezka Westwood, for your boundless energy and wisdom.

Jodi Bombardier, for your friendship, support, constant encouragement and making me believe in myself.

Eni Oken, for your belief in me and the opportunities you have given me.

Last, but by no means least, my rock Paul Thomas, for everything you have done to enable me to write this book. From making sure I didn't miss meals, to calming the panics, helping with editing and even designs - I couldn't have done it without you!

Dedication
For my Grandpa, Frank Paton. Always in my heart.

INDEX   Project names are in italics